SCHOOL
NIGHT

KATE McMILLAN

PHOTOGRAPHS BY ERIN KUNKEL

weldon**owen**

CONTENTS

SCHOOL NIGHT DINNERS

Looking for a surefire way to liven up your weeknight dinners while keeping them quick and easy to prepare? This book brings you more than 50 family-pleasing recipes that will make even the pickiest eater happy. *School Night* is the answer to turning hectic mealtimes into relaxed gatherings.

In the following pages, you'll find such cook-pleasing ideas as serve-yourself dinners, including Kabob Night and The No-Salad Salad Bar, plus five chapters filled with recipes ideal for home cooks with busy schedules. Meatless Monday offers satisfying dishes starring vegetables, from Thai Pumpkin Curry to Sesame Soba Noodles with Tofu & Sugar Snap Peas. Both kids and adults will love the recipes in Breakfast for Dinner, such as Ham & Cheese Buckwheat Waffle Sandwiches and Baked Eggs with Tomatoes, Mozzarella & Oregano.

The Make Ahead chapter highlights dishes made up of components that can be cooked ahead and then served within minutes, like Dilly Salmon Cakes with Lemony Sour Cream and Moroccan Lamb Meatballs with Spiced Tomato Sauce. Throughout the book, you'll find plenty of additional tips on how to plan ahead that will not only save you time and money but also make it possible to whip up imaginative and tasty meals every night of the week. On those nights when you just can't plan ahead, turn to The Short List, which features recipes that call for no more than a handful of ingredients, most of them pantry staples. But as simple as these dishes are, they are still big on flavor, as Spanish Tortilla with Chorizo proves.

Keeping cleanup to a minimum and prep time short is the theme of Sheet Pan Dinners, one-pan meals like Roasted Chicken with Beets, Greens & Apples and Sausage & Brussels Sprouts Bake with Spicy Mustard. And Simple Desserts is a collection of time-savvy sweet endings, such as Homemade Chocolate Pudding with Strawberry Dippers, Apple Filo Tart, and Baked Cinnamon Pears with Caramel Sauce.

With *School Night* as your guide, you will be able to create healthful, delicious, easy-to-prepare dinners that everyone at the table—including the cook—will enjoy.

ANATOMY OF A SCHOOL NIGHT DINNER

A successful school-night dinner should be easy to cook, full of flavor, and nutritious. The best way to create meals that meet these goals is to keep a well-stocked kitchen. Use the information that follows as a guide to grocery shopping, maintaining kitchen staples, and putting together foolproof meals Monday through Friday. The formula for a great school-night meal is as simple as using one or two ingredients from each of the categories below.

GRAINS & STARCHES

Whether served as the base of a dish, as a side dish to round out a menu, or for soaking up a sauce, grains and starches are important components in school night dinners. Rice, farro, bulgur, and other longer-cooking grains can be prepared in quantity and frozen in small batches for nights when time is limited. Italian and Asian noodles, which come in many shapes and sizes and in gluten-free versions, are great quick-cooking options. Peas, corn, winter squashes, and such root vegetables as potatoes, yams, and carrots are all nutritious options for adding starch to a menu.

PRODUCE

Vegetables and fruits always taste best and are highest in nutrition when they're fresh and in season. It's important to keep fresh salad greens on hand at all times if you can, plus a seasonal fruit and vegetable. But several frozen vegetables, such as spinach, peas, carrots, and broccoli, are lifesavers for when you just don't have time to shop. You can add any of these to casseroles and pasta dishes, and use them to make quick soups or sauces. And using frozen fruit in recipes is a great time-saver for speedy desserts.

FLAVOR AGENTS

Condiments, fresh and dried herbs, and spices—all of which add richness, flavor, and color—are the unsung heroes of school night dinners. These flavor agents can transform simple foods into memorably tasty ones. For example, fresh cilantro, onion, and lime will quickly turn a can of black beans into a zesty side dish. Green onions, fresh ginger, and Asian sesame oil will add zing to a pot of rice. Always keep these basic flavor enhancers on hand to liven up your menus: oil, vinegar, salt, pepper, garlic, lemons, and two or three fresh or dried herbs, such as fresh parsley and dried thyme.

PROTEIN

Meat, eggs, nuts, cheese, quinoa—these are just some of the ways to add protein to school night dinners. Protein provides essential fuel for the body, and most sources of it can be stored for a relatively long time. Canned beans and fish, for example, have a shelf life of a few years, so it's a good idea to keep a variety of canned beans and a few cans of tuna and sardines in your pantry for last-minute meals. Shrimp, fish, meat, poultry, and nuts can be kept frozen for a few months, and hard cheeses and eggs will last for a few weeks in the refrigerator.

SCHOOL NIGHT DINNER PRIMER

Perfecting your weeknight cooking skills is easy to do. The following tips and strategies will help you get dinner on the table faster and make dinner on a school night more enjoyable for you and your family.

MEAL PLAN To save both money and time, plan a week's worth of meals before you go shopping, always keeping your family's schedule in mind. For the busiest night of the week, put together a menu that can be prepared and frozen in advance, so all you'll have to do is heat it. Aim to serve at least two meals during the week that use similar ingredients, so you can prep for those meals at the same time. At the end of the week, serve an "all hands on deck" meal (see page 12) based on leftovers and pantry staples.

PREP STEP Not surprisingly, the easiest way to save time during the week is to do as much as you can in advance. Prepare a few basic foods on Sunday to store in the refrigerator or freezer. For example, make a big pot of brown rice, quinoa, or farro to round out meals all week long. Some produce can be readied in advance: Rinse herbs and greens, dry thoroughly, wrap loosely in paper towels, and store in sealable plastic bags in the fridge. Rinse and chop carrots, cauliflower, bell peppers, broccoli, and other vegetables, then store in sealable plastic bags in the fridge for 3–4 days before using.

STOCK RIGHT Keeping pantry staples and frozen foods on hand is essential to easy school-night suppers. But overstocking your kitchen with perishable foods can lead to waste and to a refrigerator that has to work too hard to keep what's inside cold. (A packed freezer, in contrast, saves energy, because the foods help keep one another frozen.) So before you load up on meats, fish, and produce, take a careful inventory of your fridge and make a meal plan for when the foods you have will be used.

MAKE MORE Whenever you are making one of your family's favorite main courses, prepare a double batch and freeze half for a later date. Do the same with side dishes, and serve them for dinner later in the week or for a brown-bag lunch the next day.

FREEZE IT Homemade frozen meals are invaluable on busy school nights. Two important tips for freezing homemade food are (1) make sure that the food has cooled completely before you cover it (to do this quickly, nest the uncovered container in an ice bath until the food is cool, then cover and transfer to the freezer); and (2) freeze in smaller portions, such as one or two servings.

THAW IT The best way to thaw frozen food is to transfer it from the freezer to the refrigerator 1–2 days before you need it. You can also thaw it in a microwave, according to the manufacturer's instructions, or warm it gently on the stove top or in the oven. If using the microwave, stove top, or oven method, always immediately cook the food once it has thawed. Never thaw food at room temperature, as harmful bacteria can develop on the surface.

TOOLS FOR SUCCESS

These basic tools will make weeknight cooking a snap.

MASKING TAPE & PERMANENT MARKER Label food (item and date) in the order it will be eaten. Note family favorites for next time.

SHARP KNIVES Purchase only good-quality knives and keep them sharp to make chopping, slicing, and dicing easier and faster.

BLENDER Use this handy appliance to make quick work of everything from smoothies and sauces to dressings, dips, soups, and more.

NONSTICK SHEET PANS Select heavy-gauge rimmed baking sheets that will stand up to high heat. A single sheet pan can accommodate an entire meal for quick cleanup.

STORAGE CONTAINERS Stock up on an array of airtight plastic and/or glass containers and jars to use when making more to store or for stashing leftovers.

BIG, HEAVY-BOTTOMED PAN Invest in a high-quality pot for cooking soups, stews, and chili. The thicker base helps prevent foods and thawing sauces from scorching.

CALENDAR & SHOPPING LIST Assemble a menu, write it on the calendar, and then use the menu to create your shopping list, adding staples and pantry items as needed.

BRINGING IT ALL TOGETHER

With the help of some pantry staples and no-cook ingredients picked up at the store, you can turn out a delicious and nutritious dinner in no time. Here are some guaranteed ways to make new favorite family suppers.

"ALL HANDS ON DECK"

Prep the fixings, lay them out in self-serve fashion, and let everyone be creative. This is an excellent way to share the dinner prep and foster lively conversation at mealtime. It will also introduce kids to new ingredients and flavors and teach them some cooking basics. Here are six easy-to-execute ideas:

GRILLED CHEESE NIGHT Put out sliced bread (such as sourdough, multigrain, and rye), cheeses (such as Cheddar, provolone, and Brie), sliced meats (such as salami, smoked turkey, and prosciutto), and a variety of toppings (such as jalapeños, olives, peperoncini, fresh and sun-dried tomatoes, arugula, and Dijon and honey mustards). Invite diners to assemble their own sandwiches. Melt 2 teaspoons unsalted butter in a large frying pan over medium heat. Cook the sandwiches, one at a time, until the bread is crispy and the cheese melts, about 4 minutes on each side.

BAKED POTATO BAR Bake potatoes and/or yams in a 425°F (220°C) oven until they can be easily pierced with a knife, about 45 minutes. Meanwhile, set out sour cream, shredded cheese, sliced green onions, leftover chili, bite-size fried bacon pieces, chopped steamed broccoli, sautéed spinach, and caramelized onions or leeks. You can even offer fried or poached eggs. Line up the hot potatoes alongside the toppings.

SIMPLE SUSHI Make a large pot of steamed rice, drizzle and then toss with a little rice vinegar, and place on the table. Lay out dried seaweed (nori) squares; smoked salmon, cooked crabmeat, grilled shrimp, or teriyaki chicken; sliced cucumber and avocado; jarred pickled ginger; prepared wasabi; and soy sauce. Invite diners to use the seaweed to roll up their favorite combinations or to assemble the ingredients as a deconstructed sushi bowl. Complete the menu with a big bowl of edamame.

BREAKFAST BURRITO BAR Lay out warmed corn or flour tortillas, shredded lettuce, homemade or jarred salsa, sliced avocado, pitted black olives, sour cream, cheeses (such as shredded pepper jack and crumbled *queso fresca*), beans (such as refried and black beans), scrambled eggs, cooked ground turkey seasoned with cumin, and fresh cilantro. Invite diners to create their own burritos or deconstructed burrito bowls.

THE NO-SALAD SALAD BAR Instead of the raw vegetables and cold cooked beans found at the typical salad bar, create this unexpected take on serve-yourself salad. Set out a cooked and cooled grain (such as farro, quinoa, or couscous), shredded rotisserie chicken or cooked and sliced mild sausages; chopped hard-boiled eggs; cut-up leftover roasted vegetables; cheese (such as crumbled feta or fresh goat cheese); canned artichoke hearts or hearts of palm, drained and rinsed; dried cranberries or apricots; pistachios or sunflower seeds; arugula or young spinach; and a simple vinaigrette of 3 parts oil and 1 part vinegar.

KABOB NIGHT Preheat a grill for direct-heat cooking and lightly oil the grate. Set out cherry tomatoes; button mushrooms; blanched baby potatoes; 1-inch (2.5-cm) pieces of zucchini, eggplant, bell pepper, broccoli, and tofu; 1-inch cubes of raw chicken or whole shrimp; and a stack of skewers (soaked if using wooden skewers). Invite diners to assemble their own skewers (adults can skewer chicken or shrimp for children), place them on the grill, and grill until the vegetables are tender and the chicken or shrimp is cooked through, about 5 minutes on each side. Serve with your favorite dipping sauce or brush with vinaigrette.

MEATLESS MONDAY

3 tablespoons olive oil

2 small red onions, halved and cut into 1-inch (2.5-cm) pieces

Kosher salt and freshly ground pepper

2 tablespoons balsamic vinegar

1 small bunch Swiss chard, stemmed and cut into 1-inch (2.5-cm) pieces

All-purpose flour for rolling

1 sheet frozen puff pastry (half of a 17 oz/ 530 g package), thawed

¼ lb (125 g) Gorgonzola cheese, crumbled

1 large egg, lightly beaten

BALSAMIC-RED ONION, CHARD & GORGONZOLA TART

Preheat the oven to 400°F (200°C).

Warm 2 tablespoons of the olive oil in a frying pan over high heat. Add the onions and sauté until soft, about 4 minutes. Reduce the heat to low and season with salt and pepper. Cook slowly, stirring occasionally, until the onions turn a deep brown, about 10 minutes. Add the balsamic vinegar and cook until the liquid is absorbed, about 2 minutes longer. Transfer the onions to a bowl.

Return the pan to medium-high heat; do not wipe the pan clean. Warm the remaining 1 tablespoon olive oil and add the chard. Season with salt and pepper and sauté, tossing the chard to coat in the oil, just until beginning to wilt, about 3 minutes. Transfer to the bowl with the onions, toss to combine, and let cool.

On a floured work surface, roll out the puff pastry into a 10-by-14-inch (25-by-35-cm) rectangle. Fold over 1 inch (2.5 cm) of each side of the dough to create a border. Fold the dough gently in half and center it over a baking sheet lined with parchment paper. Gently unfold the dough onto the baking sheet.

Prick the dough all over with the tines of a fork. Distribute the chard and onion mixture evenly around the tart and top with the cheese, leaving the borders uncovered. Brush the borders of the tart with the egg. Bake until golden brown, 22–25 minutes. Let cool slightly, then cut into squares and serve.

SERVES 4

EASY AS PIE

This tart looks impressive, but really it comes together quickly and easily. Vary it by using other toppings, such as roasted fennel, tomatoes, and black olives or zucchini, feta, and thyme. The tart can be made a day ahead, refrigerated, and served at room temperature or rewarmed gently in a 350°F (180°C) oven. Cut it into smaller squares for a terrific party appetizer.

Kosher salt and freshly ground pepper

1 cup (5 oz/155 g) polenta

¾ lb (375 g) butternut squash, peeled, seeded, and cubed

½ lb (250 g) brussels sprouts, halved

3 tablespoons olive oil

1 tablespoon balsamic vinegar

1 tablespoon unsalted butter

¾ cup (3 oz/90 g) shredded fontina cheese

2 tablespoons freshly grated Parmesan cheese

Fresh parsley leaves, chopped

CHEESY POLENTA WITH ROASTED VEGETABLES

BUDGET-FRIENDLY FAVORITE

>>>>>>>>>>>

A warm bowl of creamy polenta is about as comforting as it gets. Not only is it a filling dish, it's also inexpensive, and uncooked polenta has a long shelf life. To make the polenta ahead of time, follow the method in the recipe, using only 4 cups (32 fl oz/1 l) water, then pour the cooked polenta into a baking dish and let set in the refrigerator. Just before serving, simply rewarm the polenta in the oven, or cut it into triangles, brush with olive oil, and warm in a grill pan or frying pan.

Preheat the oven to 450°F (230°C).

In a large pot, bring 5 cups (40 fl oz/1.25 l) of water and ½ teaspoon of salt to a boil over high heat. Stir in the polenta and bring to a boil. Reduce the heat to low and cook, stirring often, until the polenta is soft and smooth, about 40 minutes.

Meanwhile, pile the squash and brussels sprouts on a baking sheet lined with parchment paper. Drizzle with the olive oil and balsamic vinegar, season well with salt and pepper, and toss to coat. Spread the vegetables into a single layer and roast, stirring once about halfway through, until fork-tender and golden brown, 20–25 minutes. Remove from the oven and set aside while you finish the polenta.

Once the polenta is soft, stir in the butter and cheeses until melted. Season to taste with salt and pepper. Spoon polenta into bowls, top with the roasted vegetables, and sprinkle chopped parsley over the top. Serve right away.

SERVES 4

WHAT YOU NEED

1½ lb (750 g) baby carrots, peeled

3 tablespoons olive oil

Kosher salt and freshly ground pepper

1 cup (8 oz/250 g) quinoa

3 blood oranges

10 oz (315 g) baby spinach leaves

¾ cup (4 oz/125 g) shelled edamame

⅓ cup (1½ oz/45 g) hazelnuts, toasted and chopped

5 oz (155 g) ricotta salata

BLOOD ORANGE VINAIGRETTE

Juice of 2 blood oranges

2 tablespoons red wine vinegar

2 teaspoons Dijon mustard

Kosher salt and freshly ground pepper

¼ cup (2 fl oz/60 ml) olive oil

QUINOA SALAD WITH ROASTED CARROTS & BLOOD ORANGES

Preheat the oven to 400°F (200°C). Pile the carrots on a baking sheet lined with parchment paper. Drizzle with the 3 tablespoons olive oil, season with salt and pepper, and toss to coat. Spread the carrots in a single layer and roast, stirring once halfway through, until fork-tender, about 15 minutes. Remove from the oven and set aside.

To make the vinaigrette, in a bowl, combine the blood orange juice, vinegar, mustard, and salt and pepper to taste. Pour in the olive oil slowly, whisking until well blended. Taste and adjust the seasoning. Set aside.

Place the quinoa and 2 cups (16 fl oz/500 ml) water in a saucepan over high heat and bring to a boil. Reduce the heat to low, cover, and simmer until the water is absorbed, 15–20 minutes. Remove the lid and fluff the quinoa with a fork.

While the quinoa is cooking, section the blood oranges: Working over a bowl with 1 blood orange at a time and using a sharp paring knife, pare away the peels and pith. Carefully cut between the membranes of the blood orange to release each orange section. Let the sections and juice fall into the bowl as you work.

In a large bowl, toss the warm quinoa with the spinach. Pour in half of the dressing and toss to coat all the ingredients well. Taste and add more dressing as needed. To assemble, mound the quinoa-spinach mixture on a platter and top with the roasted carrots, blood orange sections, edamame, and hazelnuts. With a vegetable peeler, shave the ricotta salata and scatter over the top. Serve right away.

SERVES 4

NOT JUST ANY SALAD

The mix of delicious and flavorful ingredients in this salad make it a special vegetarian dinner. Quinoa adds protein and the vegetables add color and flavor. Either fresh or frozen edamame can be used here, and there's no need to blanch them. Ricotta salata, an aged ricotta, is a salty, crumbly cheese. If you can't find it, substitute feta. If blood oranges aren't in season, simply use regular oranges.

1 lb (500 g) extra-firm tofu

Kosher salt

¾ lb (375 g) soba noodles

1 lb (500 g) sugar snap peas, trimmed

¼ cup (2 fl oz/60 ml) rice vinegar

3 tablespoons reduced-sodium soy sauce

3 tablespoons canola oil

1 tablespoon honey

2¼ teaspoons sesame oil

2-inch (5-cm) piece of fresh ginger, peeled and grated

1 clove garlic, minced

2 green onions, light and dark green parts only, sliced

1 tablespoon toasted sesame seeds

SESAME SOBA NOODLES WITH TOFU & SUGAR SNAP PEAS

TOMORROW'S LUNCH

→→→→→→→→

Here's a dish that has it all: kid-pleasing noodles, light protein, and a green vegetable! Because this dish is excellent served cold and makes a wonderful lunch-box addition, consider doubling the recipe. To mix things up, substitute halved hard-boiled eggs for the tofu and sautéed kale for the snap peas.

Place the tofu on a plate lined with 3 paper towels. Cover the tofu with 3 more paper towels and another plate. Place something very heavy, such as a pot, on top of the plate and let the tofu sit for 5 minutes. Replace both sets of paper towels and let the tofu sit for 5 minutes longer. Cut tofu into ¼-inch (6-mm) cubes and set aside.

Bring a large pot of generously salted water to a boil over medium-high heat. Add the noodles and cook according to the package directions. Drain well in a colander, rinse under cold water, tossing as you rinse until water runs clear, and drain again. Set aside.

Bring another pot of generously salted water to a boil over high heat. Add the sugar snap peas and cook just until bright green and tender-crisp, 1–2 minutes. Drain, rinse under cold water, and drain again. Set aside.

In a large bowl, stir together the rice vinegar, soy sauce, 2 tablespoons of the canola oil, the honey, 2 teaspoons of the sesame oil, the ginger, and garlic.

Warm the remaining 1 tablespoon canola oil and the remaining ¼ teaspoon sesame oil in a nonstick frying pan over medium-high heat. Add the tofu and sauté until golden on all sides, about 6 minutes.

Transfer the tofu to the bowl with the dressing, add the noodles and sugar snap peas, and toss to coat well. Add the green onions and sesame seeds and toss again. Serve warm or at room temperature or cover and refrigerate for 2 hours or up to 24 hours and serve chilled.

SERVES 4–6

2 red bell peppers, seeded and cut into 1-inch (2.5-cm) strips

2 portobello mushrooms, stemmed and halved

1 zucchini, cut into ¼-inch (6-mm) rounds

5 tablespoons (3 fl oz/80 ml) olive oil

2 tablespoons red wine vinegar

Kosher salt and freshly ground pepper

Four ½-inch (12-mm) slices crusty Italian bread, cut on the diagonal

1 clove garlic, halved lengthwise

HERBED GOAT CHEESE

¼ lb (125 g) goat cheese, at room temperature

2 tablespoons chopped fresh basil

3 tablespoons heavy cream

VEGETABLE & HERBED GOAT CHEESE BRUSCHETTA

YEAR-ROUND EASE

This recipe can be varied throughout the year depending on what's in season. Try it with roasted beets or cubes of sage-dusted butternut squash in the winter. Asparagus or mashed fava beans work beautifully in spring. Whatever you serve, pile the vegetables high and serve with a fork and knife.

In a nonreactive bowl, toss the bell peppers, mushrooms, and zucchini with 4 tablespoons (2 fl oz/60 ml) of the olive oil and the vinegar. Season well with salt and pepper, toss again, and set aside.

Warm a grill pan or frying pan over high heat.

Brush both sides of the bread with the remaining 1 tablespoon olive oil and place on the grill pan. Cook until nicely grill-marked on both sides, 2–3 minutes per side. Transfer to a plate and rub one side of each slice with the cut side of the garlic. Set aside.

Working in batches to avoid crowding, place the vegetables in the grill pan and cook until nicely grill-marked, about 3 minutes per side for the zucchini, 4 minutes per side for the mushrooms, and 5 minutes per side for the bell peppers. Transfer the vegetables to a plate as they're done and let cool slightly.

To make the herbed goat cheese, stir together the goat cheese, basil, and cream in a small bowl. Season with salt and pepper.

To assemble, slather each bruschetta with herbed goat cheese and top with grilled vegetables. Serve right away with a fork and knife, passing extra vegetables at the table.

SERVES 4

WHAT YOU NEED

2 leeks

1 bunch kale

3 tablespoons olive oil

2 carrots, chopped

1 rib celery, chopped

Kosher salt and freshly ground pepper

2 tomatoes, chopped

3 fresh thyme sprigs

2 cloves garlic, chopped

1 bay leaf

3 cans (15 oz/470 g each) cannellini beans, rinsed and drained

4 cups (32 fl oz/1 l) vegetable broth

1 tablespoon tomato paste

2 tablespoons unsalted butter

1 cup (2 oz/60 g) fresh bread crumbs

WHITE BEAN & KALE CASSOULET WITH BUTTERY BREAD CRUMBS

Using the white and light green parts only, halve the leeks lengthwise and slice. Stem the kale, including tough center spines, and cut into 1-inch (2.5-cm) pieces.

Warm the olive oil in a large heavy-bottomed saucepan over medium-high heat. Add the leeks, carrots, and celery, season with salt and pepper, and sauté until the vegetables are soft, about 6 minutes. Add the kale, tossing it to coat in the oil, and cook until beginning to wilt, about 1 minute. Add the tomatoes, thyme, garlic, and bay leaf and cook just until the tomatoes begin to release their juices, 4–5 minutes. Add the beans, vegetable broth, and tomato paste, stir to combine, and bring to a boil. Reduce the heat to low and simmer until the broth thickens, 35–40 minutes. Discard the bay leaf and thyme sprigs and season with salt and pepper.

Meanwhile, make the bread crumbs. Melt the butter in a small frying pan over medium-high heat. Stir in the bread crumbs, season with salt and pepper, and toast, stirring occasionally, about 4 minutes.

Ladle the cassoulet into bowls and top with the bread crumbs. Serve right away.

SERVES 4–6

HOMEMADE TOPPING

You won't miss meat with this easy vegetarian dinner. Tender leeks, pungent garlic, aromatic bay leaf, and rich tomato paste add big flavor. Resist the urge to buy bread crumbs at the store. All you need for homemade crumbs is 1–2 slices of day-old or toasted bread. Tear the bread into small pieces and put the bread in a food processor fitted with a metal blade. Pulse until fine bread crumbs form. This extra effort yields fresher flavor and is worth the small amount of time.

WHAT YOU NEED

1¼ lb pumpkin, cut into 1-inch (2.5-cm) cubes (about 4 cups)

2 tablespoons canola or vegetable oil

1 small yellow onion, cut into large chunks

1 red bell pepper, seeded and cut into 1-inch (2.5-cm) pieces

Kosher salt and freshly ground pepper

2½ tablespoons yellow or red curry paste

1 can (13 oz/410 g) unsweetened coconut milk

1 cup (8 fl oz/250 ml) low-sodium vegetable broth

¼ cup (¼ oz/7 g) fresh basil leaves

Steamed rice for serving

THAI PUMPKIN CURRY

Bring a large pot of generously salted water to a boil over high heat. Add the pumpkin and cook until soft but not completely cooked, about 5 minutes. Drain well and set aside.

Warm the canola oil in a heavy-bottomed saucepan over medium-high heat. Add the onion and bell pepper, season with salt and pepper, and sauté until soft, stirring occasionally, about 6 minutes. Add the pumpkin and curry paste, stir until the vegetables are well coated with the curry paste, and cook for 2 minutes longer.

Add the coconut milk and vegetable broth and bring to a boil. Reduce the heat to low and simmer until the pumpkin is fork-tender but still holds its shape, about 15 minutes. Stir in the basil and season to taste with salt and pepper. Ladle into bowls over steamed rice and serve right away.

SERVES 4-6

ANYTIME MEAL

Flavorful and filling curry comes together quickly and can be made a few days ahead of time and stored in the refrigerator. If pumpkin isn't in season, you can substitute just about any starchy vegetable, such as acorn squash or yams. Serve over steamed white or brown rice, and finish the meal with green beans sautéed in a bit of canola oil and a few drops of sesame oil.

1 lb (500 g) asparagus, tough woody ends trimmed, cut into 1-inch (2.5-cm) pieces

Up to 4 cups (32 fl oz/1 l) low-sodium vegetable broth

2 tablespoons olive oil

2 shallots, minced

2 cloves garlic, minced

1 cup (7¼ oz/230 g) farro

½ cup (4 fl oz/125 ml) dry white wine

1 can (14 oz/440 g) artichoke hearts, drained thoroughly and quartered

2 tablespoons fresh parsley leaves, chopped

2 tablespoons fresh basil leaves, chopped

Kosher salt and freshly ground pepper

¼ cup (1 oz/30 g) freshly grated Parmesan cheese

ASPARAGUS, ARTICHOKE & HERB FARROTTO

A HEALTHIER RISOTTO

Farrotto is the name for risotto made with farro, a delicious and nutritious grain. First, the farro is toasted in a skillet and then warmed broth is added in increments until the mixture is creamy. *Farrotto* is best served fresh from the pot, but if you want to rewarm it, you can add warmed broth (try ¼ cup/2 fl oz/60 ml at a time). Serve with a warm baguette and a chunk of Parmesan cheese.

Bring a large pot of generously salted water to a boil over high heat. Add the asparagus and cook until tender-crisp, about 2 minutes. Drain, rinse under cold water, and drain again. Set aside.

Warm the broth in a small saucepan over low heat.

Warm the olive oil in a large saucepan over medium-high heat. Add the shallots and sauté until soft, about 3 minutes. Add the garlic and cook until softened, about 1 minute more. Stir in the farro and toast, stirring often, for about 3 minutes. Add the wine and simmer until the liquid reduces by half, about 1 minute.

Reduce the heat to medium. Using a ladle, add about ½ cup (4 fl oz/125 ml) of the warm broth at a time, stirring often and allowing each addition to be absorbed before adding the next ladleful of broth. This process will take about 40 minutes.

When the farro is just shy of al dente, add the asparagus, artichoke hearts, and the last ladleful of broth. Cook, stirring occasionally, until the vegetables are heated through and just tender, about 3 minutes. Remove the pan from the heat, stir in the cheese and herbs, season with salt and pepper, and serve right away.

SERVES 4-6

WHAT YOU NEED

1 lb (500 g) carrots, shredded

3 large eggs, lightly beaten

¾ cup (4 oz/125 g) almond flour

⅓ cup (½ oz/15 g) minced fresh parsley

2 cloves garlic, minced

Kosher salt and freshly ground pepper

Unsalted butter for frying

2 tablespoons olive oil

1 tablespoon sherry vinegar

Juice of ½ lime

½ teaspoon ground cumin

5 oz (155 g) arugula, tough stems removed

½ lb (250 g) feta cheese, crumbled

¼ cup (1 oz/30 g) pepitas or sunflower seeds

CARROT LATKES WITH ARUGULA, FETA & PEPITA SALAD

In a bowl, stir together the carrots, eggs, almond flour, parsley, and garlic. Season well with salt and pepper.

Preheat the oven to 200°F (95°C).

Warm ½ tablespoon of butter in a nonstick frying pan over medium heat. Using your hands, use ¼ cup (2 oz/60 g) of the carrot mixture to form a mound, then slightly flatten it until it's ¼ inch (6 mm) thick. Do not flatten the latke in the pan or it will fall apart. Working in batches to avoid crowding, place the latkes in the pan and cook until lightly browned on both sides, about 3 minutes per side. Transfer to a baking sheet and keep warm in the oven until ready to serve. Repeat until all the latkes are cooked.

In a large bowl, stir together the olive oil, sherry vinegar, lime juice, and cumin. Season with salt and pepper. Add the arugula and toss well to make sure that each leaf is nicely coated. Add the feta and pepitas and gently toss just to combine.

Place the latkes on plates with the arugula salad. Serve right away.

SERVES 4

A GLUTEN-FREE TREAT

Almond flour is a terrific gluten-free alternative to all-purpose flour, as is coconut flour. You can also make this recipe with shredded zucchini or potatoes in place of the carrots. The batter can be made a day ahead, but serve the latkes hot from the pan for the best results. Do not fuss with the latkes once they are in the pan; they need time to form a browned exterior, or they will crumble.

BREAKFAST FOR DINNER

WHAT YOU NEED

1 cup (5 oz/155 g) buckwheat flour

1 cup (5 oz/155 g) all-purpose flour

2 tablespoons sugar

2 teaspoons baking powder

¼ teaspoon kosher salt

1½ cups (12 fl oz/375 ml) whole milk

½ cup (4 fl oz/125 ml) canola oil

2 large eggs

¾ lb (375 g) sliced Virginia or Black Forest ham

2 cups (½ lb/250 g) shredded Cheddar cheese

2 small tomatoes, sliced (optional)

HAM & CHEESE BUCKWHEAT WAFFLE SANDWICHES

In a bowl, whisk together the flours, sugar, baking powder, and salt. Add the milk, canola oil, and eggs and whisk until smooth. Set aside.

Preheat a waffle iron. Coat lightly with cooking spray. According to the manufacturer's directions, pour the batter into the iron and close the lid. Cook until the waffle is golden brown, about 3 minutes. Repeat with the remaining batter.

Preheat the broiler. Line a baking sheet with aluminum foil. Break or cut the waffles into quarters. Place half of the waffle pieces on the baking sheet and top with the ham and cheese, dividing them evenly. Slip under the broiler about 4 inches (10 cm) from the heat source and broil until the cheese melts, about 2 minutes. Remove from the broiler.

Top each sandwich with a tomato slice, if desired, and a waffle piece. Serve right away.

SERVES 4–6

WONDERFUL WAFFLES

Despite its name, buckwheat is actually not a type of wheat. But it adds a really wonderful nutty flavor to these savory waffles. For a variation, chop the ham and stir it, along with the grated cheese, into the batter. Serve the waffles lightly buttered, with a mixed-fruit salad alongside.

1 teaspoon distilled white vinegar

10 large eggs

½ cup (4 fl oz/125 ml) whole milk

6 slices day-old French bread

1 tablespoon unsalted butter

¾ cup (3 oz/90 g) freshly grated
Parmesan cheese

¼ lb (125 g) sliced prosciutto

BLENDER HOLLANDAISE

18 tablespoons (9 oz/280 g) unsalted butter,
melted and slightly cooled

2 large egg yolks

2 tablespoons fresh lemon juice

Pinch of cayenne pepper

Kosher salt

Roasted asparagus for serving (see note)

PARMESAN FRENCH TOAST WITH BLENDER HOLLANDAISE

ROASTED ASPARAGUS

>>>>>>>>>>

To make the roasted asparagus, preheat the oven to 425°F (220°C). Pile 1 lb (500 g) asparagus, tough woody ends trimmed, on a baking sheet lined with parchment paper. Drizzle with 1 tablespoon olive oil, season well with kosher salt and freshly ground pepper, and toss to coat. Spread the asparagus in a single layer and roast until fork-tender, 6–8 minutes.

Line a plate with paper towels. Fill a wide frying pan with 1 inch (2.5 cm) of water, add the vinegar, and bring to a boil over medium heat. Reduce the heat to low so that the water gently simmers. One at a time, break 6 of the eggs into a ramekin or small bowl and carefully slip the eggs into the water. Using a tablespoon, occasionally spoon the hot water over the tops of the eggs as they cook. Cook until the eggs are set but the yolks are still runny, about 5 minutes. Using a slotted spoon, carefully transfer the eggs to the prepared plate. Set aside.

In a bowl, whisk together the remaining 4 eggs and the milk. Pour the egg mixture into a large, shallow baking dish. Add the bread and let stand until the bread soaks up some of the egg mixture, about 4 minutes per side. While the bread soaks, make the hollandaise. Put the melted butter in a glass measuring pitcher. Combine the egg yolks, lemon juice, and cayenne in a blender. Blend until well combined and the mixture turns pale yellow, 30–40 seconds. With the blender running, add just a couple drops of the melted butter, slowly adding more until it's a steady stream. Blend until the hollandaise is thick and smooth, 1–2 minutes. Season to taste with salt and set aside.

Melt the 1 tablespoon butter in a nonstick frying pan over medium heat. Remove the bread from the egg mixture, letting the excess liquid drip back into the baking dish, and place the bread in the pan. Cook until the bottoms are golden brown, about 4 minutes. Flip and immediately top the bread with the cheese. Cook until the cheese melts and the other sides are golden brown, about 4 minutes longer.

To assemble, top each piece of French toast with 1–2 prosciutto slices, a few asparagus spears, a poached egg, and a generous helping of hollandaise. Serve right away.

SERVES 6

WHAT YOU NEED

5 tablespoons (2½ oz/75 g) unsalted butter

2 tablespoons all-purpose flour

1 cup (8 fl oz/250 ml) whole milk

¼ cup (1 oz/30 g) freshly grated
Parmesan cheese

⅛ teaspoon freshly grated nutmeg

Kosher salt and freshly ground pepper

8 slices sourdough bread

½ lb (250 g) sliced Virginia or Black Forest ham

½ cup (2 oz/60 g) shredded Gruyère cheese

4 large eggs

CROQUE MADAME

FRENCH FOR DINNER

A croque madame is the French version of a grilled ham and cheese sandwich, with a fried egg on top. This delicious sandwich is a great way to use up day-old bread and last bits of cheese. Serve with a simple salad of butter lettuce and sliced apples, tossed with a Dijon vinaigrette.

Melt 4 tablespoons (2 oz/60 g) of the butter in a heavy-bottomed saucepan over medium heat. Add the flour to the melted butter and whisk continuously for 1 minute. Add the milk and cook, whisking often, until the mixture thickens, about 8 minutes. Stir in the Parmesan and nutmeg and remove from the heat. Season to taste with salt and pepper and set aside.

Move an oven rack to 3–4 inches (7.5–10 cm) from the broiler and preheat the broiler. Line a baking sheet with aluminum foil. Place the bread on the baking sheet. Slip under the broiler and broil until toasted, about 2 minutes per side. Remove from the broiler.

Cover 4 of the bread slices with ham, followed by 1 tablespoon of the cheese sauce, spreading it evenly with a spoon. Top each sandwich with a slice of bread, followed by the remaining sauce and the Gruyère. Broil just until the Gruyère melts and turns golden brown, about 3 minutes. Transfer the sandwiches to plates to await the eggs.

Melt the remaining 1 tablespoon butter in a nonstick frying pan over medium-high heat. Break the eggs into the pan and cook until they are set but still runny, 4–5 minutes. Using a spatula, top each sandwich with an egg. Serve right away.

SERVES 4

TOMATILLO SALSA

1 lb (500 g) tomatillos, papery husks removed

2 cloves garlic, unpeeled

1 jalapeño chile, halved lengthwise and seeded

½ white onion, chopped

½ cup (½ oz/15 g) fresh cilantro leaves

½ teaspoon kosher salt

1 tablespoon olive oil

¼ cup (1 oz/30 g) chopped white onion

1 clove garlic

1 can (14½ oz/455 g) chopped tomatoes

Kosher salt and freshly ground pepper

8 large eggs

1 tablespoon unsalted butter

Toppings and tortilla chips for serving (see note)

SCOOPABLE HUEVOS RANCHEROS WITH TOMATILLO SALSA

Move an oven rack 6 inches (15 cm) from the broiler and preheat the broiler. Line a baking sheet with aluminum foil.

To make the tomatillo salsa, rinse the tomatillos under warm water to dissolve the sticky coating of the skins. Pat dry, cut in half lengthwise, and arrange on the prepared baking sheet, cut side down. Place the garlic and jalapeño, cut side down, on the baking sheet so everything is in a single, uncrowded layer. Broil, turning everything once, until the vegetables are charred all over, about 10 minutes. Remove from the broiler and let cool.

When cool enough to handle, peel the garlic. Combine the tomatillos, garlic, jalapeño, onion, cilantro, and salt in a blender. Blend until a coarse purée forms. Set aside.

Warm the olive oil in a saucepan over medium heat. Add the onion and sauté until translucent, about 4 minutes. Add the garlic and sauté just until soft, about 1 minute longer. Stir in the tomatoes and season with salt and pepper. Raise the heat to medium-high and bring to a boil. Reduce the heat to low and simmer until the sauce darkens in color and thickens a bit, about 15 minutes. Let cool slightly.

Break the eggs into a large bowl, beat with a fork, and season with salt and pepper. Melt the butter in a large, nonstick frying pan over medium-high heat. Pour the eggs into the skillet and cook until they just begin to set, about 1 minute. Using a heatproof rubber spatula, gently stir the eggs around the pan, letting any uncooked egg run onto the bottom of the pan. Continue cooking until the eggs are completely set, about 4 minutes.

Spoon the tomato sauce on plates, top with the scrambled eggs, additional toppings (see note), and salsa. Serve right away, passing the tortilla chips at the table.

SERVES 4

TOP IT ON, SCOOP IT UP

This dish is fantastic with toppings: canned refried beans warmed on the stove top, sliced avocado, and shredded Monterey jack cheese. After spooning the tomato sauce on plates, top with the scrambled eggs and beans then layer on the avocado, cheese, and salsa. Serve alongside tortilla chips for scooping up the saucy food. (Forks optional!) The tomatillo salsa can be made up to 5 days in advance and stored in the refrigerator.

7 tablespoons (3½ fl oz/96 ml) olive oil

1 yellow onion, chopped

1 lb (500 g) Yukon gold potatoes, cut into ⅓-inch (9-mm) pieces

Kosher salt and freshly ground pepper

2 cloves garlic, minced

½ lb (250 g) cremini mushrooms, brushed clean and chopped

2 zucchini, cut into ½-inch (12-mm) pieces

1 red bell pepper, seeded and cut into ½-inch (12-mm) pieces

3 tablespoons fresh thyme, chopped

1½ tablespoons unsalted butter

6 large eggs

VEGETABLE & THYME HASH WITH FRIED EGGS

Warm 3 tablespoons of the olive oil in a large nonstick frying pan over medium-high heat. Add the onion and potatoes, season generously with salt and pepper, and sauté until the potatoes are golden brown and soft, about 12 minutes. Add the garlic and sauté just until softened, about 2 minutes longer. Transfer to a bowl.

Return the pan to medium-high heat; do not wipe the pan clean. Warm 2 tablespoons of the olive oil in the hot pan and add the mushrooms. Season with salt and pepper and sauté until the mushrooms soften and deepen in color, about 4 minutes. Transfer to the bowl with the potatoes.

Once again, return the pan to medium-high heat; do not wipe the pan clean. Warm the remaining 2 tablespoons olive oil in the hot pan and add the zucchini and bell pepper. Season with salt and pepper and sauté until just soft, about 4 minutes. Return the potatoes and mushrooms to the pan and stir to combine. Stir in the thyme and cook just until warmed through, about 2 minutes. Season to taste with salt and pepper and keep warm over low heat.

Melt the butter in a nonstick pan over medium-high heat. Break 3 eggs at time into the pan and cook until they are set but still runny, 4–5 minutes. Spoon the vegetable hash onto plates and, using a spatula, top with an egg. Serve right away.

SERVES 4–6

RECYCLED LEFTOVERS

Here's a recipe born for leftovers! This kitchen sink-style hash can be made using any vegetables you have on hand, such as leftover cooked brussels sprouts or cherry tomatoes. Cooked vegetables can be added during the last few minutes of cooking. The addition of leftover cooked steak, chicken, pork, or salmon bumps up the protein level. Serve with buttered toast or warmed croissants.

2 tablespoons olive oil

½ small yellow onion, chopped

2 cloves garlic, minced

1 can (28 oz/875 g) crushed tomatoes

Kosher salt and freshly ground pepper

4 tablespoons (2 fl oz/60 ml) heavy cream

¼ lb (125 g) fresh mozzarella cheese, drained and cut into ½-inch (12-mm) pieces

¼ cup (¼ oz/7 g) fresh oregano leaves, roughly chopped

8 large eggs

4 slices buttered toast for serving (optional)

BAKED EGGS WITH TOMATOES, MOZZARELLA & OREGANO

ASSEMBLE YOUR OWN

Baked eggs are fun for the whole family because each person can create a custom dish. Lay out the ramekins, tomato sauce, cream, cheese, oregano, and eggs in an assembly line. If you like, offer feta, fresh basil, and sautéed spinach as optional mix-ins. Place a piece of parchment paper on the baking sheet so each chef can add an identifying name.

Warm the olive oil in a heavy-bottomed saucepan over medium-high heat. Add the onion and sauté until translucent, about 5 minutes. Add the garlic and sauté until soft, about 2 minutes longer. Stir in the tomatoes with their juices, season with salt and pepper, and bring to a boil. Reduce the heat to low and simmer until nicely thickened, about 15 minutes. Season to taste and let cool.

Preheat the oven to 350°F (180°C).

Place four 4½-inch (11.5-cm) ramekins on a baking sheet. Spoon 5 tablespoons of the tomato sauce and 1 tablespoon of the heavy cream into each ramekin. Top with the mozzarella and the oregano, dividing them evenly. Break 2 eggs into each ramekin and season with salt and pepper.

Bake until the egg whites are opaque and the yolks are set but still runny in the middle, about 15 minutes. The eggs will continue to cook from the residual heat. Let cool slightly and serve with toast, if desired.

SERVES 4

1 head cauliflower, thick stems removed, cut into 1-inch (2.5-cm) florets

3 tablespoons olive oil

Kosher salt and freshly ground pepper

4 slices thick-cut bacon

2 shallots, sliced

1 tablespoon unsalted butter

2 cups (¼ lb/125 g) sourdough baguette, cut into ½-inch (12-mm) cubes

½ lb (250 g) fresh spinach leaves, tough stems removed

1½ tablespoons white wine vinegar

4 poached eggs (see page 36 for method)

BREAKFAST SALAD BOWL

POWER MEAL

>>>>>>>>>

This tasty bowl is loaded with nutrition from the vegetables and the poached egg. You can use other greens, such as kale or chard, and change up the vegetables throughout the year, substituting sweet potatoes, red bell peppers, and zucchini for the cauliflower. For a different flavor, try swapping pinto or black beans for the egg, replace the croutons with a warmed tortilla, and top the salad with fresh salsa.

Preheat the oven to 425°F (220°C). Pile the cauliflower on a baking sheet lined with parchment paper. Drizzle with 2 tablespoons of the olive oil, season well with salt and pepper, and toss to coat. Spread the cauliflower in a single layer and roast, stirring once or twice, until golden brown and fork-tender, 30–35 minutes.

In a frying pan over medium-high heat, fry the bacon until crispy, about 7 minutes. Transfer to paper towels to drain. When cool enough to handle, break the bacon into bite-sized pieces and set aside. Discard all but 1 tablespoon of the bacon grease in the pan and warm over medium-high heat. Add the shallots, season with salt and pepper, and sauté, stirring occasionally, until golden brown, about 3 minutes. Transfer the shallots to a bowl and set aside.

Melt the butter in the frying pan over medium-high heat. Allow to get hot enough to sizzle. Add the baguette and toss to coat each cube completely. Season generously with salt and pepper and sauté, stirring once or twice, until the bread is toasted, about 5 minutes. Transfer to a plate and set aside.

Remove the cauliflower from the oven and immediately pile the spinach over the top. Using tongs or a wooden spoon, toss the spinach with the hot cauliflower until the spinach just begins to wilt. Drizzle the remaining 1 tablespoon of olive oil and the vinegar over the top, add the shallots, bacon, and croutons, and toss again to combine. Season with salt and pepper.

Divide the salad among 4 bowls and top each with a poached egg. Serve right away.

SERVES 4

2 tablespoons olive oil

2 tablespoons fresh lemon juice

Kosher salt and freshly ground pepper

12 large eggs

4 tablespoons unsalted butter

12 tablespoons (3 oz/90 g) cream cheese, at room temperature

6 oz (185 g) thinly sliced smoked salmon

4 cups (¼ lb/125 g) mixed baby greens

½ cup (¾ oz/20 g) rough chopped mixed herbs, such as tarragon, basil, and parsley

SMOKED SALMON OMELET WITH MIXED HERB SALAD

Preheat the oven to 200°F (93°C). In a large bowl, whisk together the olive oil and lemon juice and season with salt and pepper. Set aside.

Break 3 of the eggs into a bowl, beat with a fork, and season with salt and pepper.

Melt 1 tablespoon of the butter in a 6-inch (15-cm) nonstick frying pan over medium heat. Pour the eggs into the pan and let cook until they just begin to set, about 2 minutes. Using a heatproof rubber spatula, gently lift up the edges to allow the uncooked eggs to run onto the bottom of the pan. Repeat this process until there are no more raw eggs. Let the omelet cook, without stirring, until cooked through, 1–2 minutes.

When the eggs are mostly set, spoon 3 tablespoons of the cream cheese and 1½ oz (45 g) of the smoked salmon over half of the omelet. Using a spatula, fold the uncovered half of the omelet over the filled half. Cook the omelet for 2 minutes longer, then slide onto a plate. Keep the cooked omelets warm in the oven. Repeat with the remaining eggs, butter, salmon, and cream cheese to make 3 more omelets.

While the last omelet is cooking, add the baby greens and herbs to the bowl of dressing. Toss to coat all the ingredients well. Top the omelets with the salad, dividing it evenly. Serve right away.

SERVES 4

VERSATILE PROTEIN

Eggs are invaluable in the kitchen, for they provide perfect single servings of protein and, in a bind, can be turned into a delicious meal for any time of day. Omelets are one of the quickest and simplest ways to use eggs. Even the most basic omelet, with nothing more than salt and pepper, is delicious and satisfying. But you can easily increase the appeal with cheese, fresh herbs, cooked vegetables or meats, and prepared salsas. A simple mixed salad on top turns any omelet into a full meal.

5 tablespoons (2½ oz/75 g) unsalted butter, plus more for greasing

1 cup (8 fl oz/250 ml) whole milk

1 cup (5 oz/155 g) all-purpose flour

2 large eggs

½ teaspoon salt

1 firm but ripe pear, quartered, cored, and thinly sliced

½ lb (250 g) Brie cheese, sliced

1 lb (500 g) sliced best-quality smoked turkey

SAUTÉED PEAR, TURKEY & BRIE CREPES

Melt 2 tablespoons of the butter in a frying pan over medium heat. In a bowl, whisk together the milk, flour, ⅓ cup (3 fl oz/80 ml) water, eggs, and salt until smooth. Stir in the melted butter. Cover and refrigerate for at least 1 hour or up to 24 hours.

In the same pan, melt 2 tablespoons of the butter over medium-high heat, until bubbly and golden brown, about 2 minutes. Add the pears, spreading them in a single layer, and cook, until golden brown on both sides, about 2 minutes on each side. The pears should be caramelized, but still hold their shape. Remove the pan from the heat and let stand while you make the crepes.

Preheat the oven to 350°F (180°C). Have ready 2 baking sheets. Warm a 6-inch (15-cm) crepe pan or nonstick frying pan over medium-high heat. Add ½ teaspoon of butter and swirl the pan until the butter melts and covers the bottom of the pan. (If you are using a seasoned crepe pan, you will need to butter the pan only once. If you are using a nonstick pan, you will need to lightly butter the pan in between crepes.) Ladle about ¼ cup (2½ oz/75 g) of the batter into the pan and tilt the pan to cover the bottom evenly. Cook until the bottom is lightly browned, 1–2 minutes. Run a fork around the edges of the pan to loosen the crepe and transfer to the baking sheet. Do not cook the other side. Repeat with the remaining batter until you have 6 crepes.

Place 1 crepe on a work surface. Place one-sixth of the Brie over one-quarter of the crepe, followed by one-sixth of the turkey and one-sixth of the pears. Repeat with the remaining crepes, Brie, turkey, and pears, dividing them evenly. Bake until the cheese is gooey but not completely melted, about 3 minutes. Remove from the oven and carefully fold each crepe in half and then in half again. Serve right away.

SERVES 6

SAVORY OR SWEET

Crepes are one of the few dishes that can serve as both dinner and dessert! Double the batter to serve with a savory topping for dinner, and then top with Nutella and sliced banana or sprinkle with sugar and lemon juice for dessert. When pears are out of season, try this recipe with strawberry or fig jam. Serve the savory crepes with a simple spinach salad alongside.

THE SHORT
LIST

1½ lb (750 g) skirt steak

Kosher salt and freshly ground pepper

1 tablespoon olive oil

1½ cups (9 oz/280 g) cherry tomatoes, preferably multicolored

2 ripe avocados

¼ cup (⅓ oz/10 g) fresh parsley leaves, chopped

Juice of ½ lime

SKIRT STEAK WITH AVOCADO & TOMATOES

STEAK FOR THE WIN

→>>>>>>>>>

Skirt steak is a weeknight favorite because it cooks in just 6–8 minutes. The most important thing to remember is that it must be sliced against the grain. For variations, swap the tomatoes for peaches or try fresh corn kernels in place of avocados. Or serve with grilled bread for open-faced steak sandwiches.

Cutting with the grain, cut the steak into a few smaller pieces. Season with salt and pepper and let stand at room temperature for 15 minutes.

Warm the olive oil in a grill pan or frying pan over high heat. Working in batches as needed to avoid crowding, add the steak and cook until medium rare, 3–4 minutes per side. Transfer the steak to a cutting board, cover loosely with aluminum foil, and let rest for 10 minutes.

Cut the cherry tomatoes in half and place in a large bowl. Pit and peel the avocados and cut into ⅓-inch (9-mm) cubes. Add to the bowl along with the parsley and the lime juice and gently toss just to combine. Season with salt and pepper to taste.

Slice the steak against the grain and place on a platter, fanning out the slices. Mound the avocado and tomato mixture alongside the steak. Serve right away.

SERVES 4–6

1 bunch broccolini, about ½ lb (250 g)

1 cup (7 ¼ oz/230 g) wheat berries

1½ tablespoons olive oil, plus more as needed

1 lb (500 g) kielbasa, cut into ½-inch (12-mm) slices

3 tomatoes, chopped

3 cloves garlic, sliced

⅓ cup (½ oz/15 g) fresh basil leaves, chopped

Kosher salt and freshly ground pepper

3 tablespoons freshly grated Parmesan cheese

WHEAT BERRIES WITH KIELBASA & BROCCOLINI

Bring a large pot of generously salted water to a boil over high heat. Add the broccolini and cook until the stems are tender-crisp, about 4 minutes. Remove the broccolini from the water and bring the water back to a boil.

Add the wheat berries to the boiling water and cook according to the package directions. Drain well and set aside. When cool enough to handle, cut the broccolini into 2-inch (5-cm) pieces. Set aside.

Warm ½ tablespoon of the olive oil in a large frying pan over medium-high heat. Add the kielbasa and cook until nicely browned on all sides, 6–8 minutes. Transfer the kielbasa to a bowl.

Return the pan to medium-high heat; do not wipe the pan clean. Add the remaining 1 tablespoon olive oil, the tomatoes, and garlic to the hot pan and sauté until the tomatoes release their juices and the garlic is soft and golden, about 4 minutes. Stir in the wheat berries, kielbasa, broccolini, and basil and season with salt and pepper. If the wheat berries seem dry, add more olive oil. Transfer to a large serving bowl, sprinkle with the Parmesan cheese, and serve right away.

SERVES 4

ONE-DISH BLISS

Wheat berries—nutty whole grains, filled with vitamins and fiber—offer a delightful crunch and hearty flavor. Smoky kielbasa and fresh broccolini turn this into a complete meal. If you can't find wheat berries, use orzo or quinoa. A dusting of freshly grated Parmesan cheese completes this flavorful one-pot meal.

¾ cup (6 fl oz/180 ml) plus 2 tablespoons olive oil

3 russet potatoes, 1¼ lb (625 g) total weight, cut into ⅓-inch (9-mm) dice

1 yellow onion, chopped

Kosher salt and freshly ground pepper

½ lb (250 g) Mexican chorizo, casings removed

4 large eggs

Sour cream for serving

SPANISH TORTILLA WITH CHORIZO

SPANISH MEETS MEXICAN

The Spanish tortilla—a classic dish reminiscent of a potato-filled frittata—gets updated here with the addition of spicy Mexican chorizo. Made with fresh pork, Mexican chorizo is uncooked and has more flavor than Spanish chorizo, which is smoked.

Warm ¾ cup (6 fl oz/180 ml) of the olive oil in a large frying pan over medium-high heat. Add the potatoes and onion, season well with salt and pepper, and cook, stirring often, until the potatoes are soft, about 15 minutes. Using a slotted spoon, transfer the potato mixture to a colander and let drain.

Return the pan to medium-high heat; do not wipe the pan clean. Add the chorizo to the hot pan and cook, stirring often and using a wooden spoon to break up any clumps, until the meat is browned and cooked through, 4–5 minutes. Using a slotted spoon, transfer to paper towels to drain.

Break the eggs into a large bowl and beat with a fork. Add the potatoes and the chorizo and stir just to combine.

Warm the remaining 2 tablespoons olive oil in a 10-inch (25-cm) nonstick frying pan over medium-low heat. Pour the egg mixture into the pan and cook, undisturbed, until the bottom is nicely browned, about 7 minutes. To check if the tortilla is ready to flip, gently slide a nonstick spatula along the edges of pan to loosen it. If the tortilla sticks to the sides of the pan or it begins to fall apart, cook it another minute or two.

To flip the tortilla, turn off the heat. Place a large plate over the top of the pan and, using potholders, carefully invert the plate and pan together, then lift off the pan to release the tortilla. Immediately slide the tortilla back into the pan to cook the other side. Return the pan to medium-low heat and cook until the egg is set and the center is firm when you shake the pan, 7–10 minutes. Slide the tortilla onto a cutting board and cut into wedges. Serve warm or at room temperature, passing sour cream at the table.

SERVES 4

⅓ cup (2 oz/60 g) dried cherries

2 tablespoons olive oil

5 oz (155 g) baby arugula

Kosher salt and freshly ground pepper

1 skin-on, boneless turkey breast
(about 2¼ lb/1 kg), butterflied

3 oz (90 g) goat cheese

¼ cup (⅓ oz/10 g) fresh basil leaves

TURKEY ROULADE WITH ARUGULA, GOAT CHEESE & CHERRIES

Preheat the oven to 375°F (190°C). Place the cherries in a small bowl and cover with hot water. Let stand for 5 minutes, then drain.

Warm 1 tablespoon of the olive oil in a large frying pan over medium-high heat. Add the arugula, season with salt and pepper, and cook, stirring occasionally, until wilted, about 2 minutes. Transfer to a bowl and let cool.

Place the turkey on a work surface, skin side down. Leaving a 1-inch (2.5-cm) border, top with the arugula, cherries, goat cheese, and basil. Roll the turkey breast up tightly lengthwise and tie with kitchen string in 4 evenly spaced spots. Season with salt and pepper.

In a large, heavy-bottomed, ovenproof frying pan, warm the remaining 1 tablespoon olive oil over medium-high heat. Add the turkey roll and cook, turning as needed, until golden brown on all sides, about 10 minutes total. Transfer the pan to the oven and bake until an instant-read thermometer inserted into the center of the roll registers 165°F (74°C), 35–45 minutes. Remove from the oven, cover loosely with aluminum foil, and let rest for 10 minutes. Snip the strings and remove carefully. Cut the roll crosswise into 1-inch (2.5-cm) roulades. Serve right away.

SERVES 4

STUFF, ROLL, COOK!

Elegant enough for company, but simple to make, a roulade takes turkey to a new level. Naturally lean turkey breast is butterflied (ask the butcher to do this for you); layered with arugula, cherries, goat cheese, and fresh basil; then rolled, seared, and baked. Make a side salad out of extra stuffing ingredients: raw arugula, cherries, goat cheese, dressed with oil and vinegar.

4 boneless pork chops, ½ inch (12 mm) thick, about 1¼ lbs (625 g) total weight

Kosher salt and freshly ground pepper

3 tablespoons olive oil

2 small red onions, halved and sliced

12 small apricots, halved and pitted or 18 dried apricot pieces

½ cup (½ oz/15 g) fresh sage leaves

3 tablespoons balsamic vinegar

PORK CHOPS WITH CARAMELIZED APRICOTS & SAGE

FLAVOR BOMB

>>>>>>>>>

This dish is packed with so much flavor, you'll be amazed that it uses so few ingredients. You can substitute other stone fruits, such as peaches and plums, for the apricots. You can also use bone-in pork chops (they will take a bit longer to cook) or buy a pork tenderloin and cut medallions yourself. Serve with roasted fingerling potatoes, couscous, or quinoa.

Season the pork chops with salt and pepper. Warm ½ tablespoon of the olive oil in a frying pan over medium-high heat. Add the pork and cook until opaque throughout and an instant-read thermometer inserted into the center of a pork chop registers 145°F (63°C), 4–6 minutes per side. Transfer the pork chops to a plate and cover loosely with aluminum foil.

Return the pan to medium-high heat; do not wipe the pan clean. Warm the remaining 2½ tablespoons olive oil in the pan. Add the onions and sauté until soft, about 4 minutes. Reduce the heat to medium-low and season with salt and pepper. Cook slowly, stirring occasionally, until the onions turn deep brown, about 10 minutes.

Raise the heat to medium and add the apricots and sage. Cook, stirring occasionally, until the apricots are soft and caramelized, about 4 minutes. Add the balsamic vinegar and cook until the liquid is absorbed, about 1 minute.

Return the pork and its juices to the pan and turn to coat each piece with the sauce. Cook just until the pork is warmed through, about 2 minutes.

Transfer the pork chops to plates and pile the onion-apricot mixture on top. Serve right away.

SERVES 4

2 tablespoons olive oil

2 shallots, minced

3 cloves garlic, minced

Kosher salt and freshly ground pepper

2 cups (16 fl oz/500 ml) dry white wine

4 lb (2 kg) mussels, scrubbed clean and debearded

¼ cup (⅓ oz/10 g) fresh parsley leaves, chopped

1 baguette, sliced, for serving

MUSSELS MARINIÈRE

FAST & FRENCH

Mussels marinière is simply mussels steamed in white wine (the alcohol is nearly cooked off in the process, but you can use vegetable broth in its place). Weeknight dinners don't get much quicker or more classy than this one. Make sure you scrub the mussels well to remove grit and sand and discard any unopened mussels before serving. To round out the meal, serve a French-style frisée or bibb lettuce salad.

Warm the olive oil in a deep pot with a tight-fitting lid over medium heat. Add the shallots and sauté until soft, about 3 minutes. Add the garlic, season with salt and pepper, and sauté for 1 minute longer. Add the wine, bring to a simmer, and add the mussels. Cover the pan and cook, shaking the pan gently a few times, until the mussels open, about 5 minutes.

Using a slotted spoon, transfer the mussels to a serving bowl and sprinkle with parsley. Discard any mussels that don't open. Ladle the broth remaining in the pot into the serving bowl. Serve right away, passing the baguette at the table.

SERVES 4

2 large eggs, lightly beaten

1½ cups (2 oz/60 g) panko bread crumbs

Kosher salt and freshly ground pepper

4 skinless tilapia fillets, about 1½ lb (750g) total weight

BUTTER-CAPER SAUCE

½ cup (¼ lb/125 g) unsalted butter

½ cup (4oz/125 g) capers, rinsed and drained

Juice of 1 lemon

PANKO-CRUSTED TILAPIA WITH BUTTER-CAPER SAUCE

Preheat the broiler. Line a baking sheet with aluminum foil.

Set up an assembly line: In a shallow bowl, beat the eggs. Put the panko in a second shallow bowl next to the eggs and season well with salt and pepper. Dip a fish fillet into the egg, letting the excess egg drip back into the bowl. Coat the fish in the panko, making sure to cover on all sides.

Place the fish on the prepared baking sheet and coat the fish with cooking spray (this will keep the panko from burning and give it a nice golden color). Slip under the broiler about 4–5 inches (10–13 cm) from the heat source and broil until golden brown, about 4 minutes. Flip the fish, coat it lightly with cooking spray again, and broil until it flakes and is opaque throughout, 4–6 minutes longer.

While the fish cooks, make the butter-caper sauce. Melt the butter in a small pan over medium heat until bubbly and golden brown, about 4 minutes. Add the capers and cook just until warmed through, about 1 minute. Remove from the heat, stir in the lemon juice, and season with pepper.

Transfer the fish to plates and spoon the sauce on top. Serve right away.

SERVES 4

BREADED & CRISP

Panko—Japanese-style bread crumbs—gives fish a nice and flavorful crunch. You can use any type of fish you'd like and adjust the cooking time depending on how thick the fish is. For the freshest, crispiest fish, don't buy fish more than 24 hours before using, and wait to spoon the sauce over the fish until just before serving. Round out the meal with sautéed spinach and roasted carrots.

1½ cups (9 oz/280 g) Israeli couscous

4 tablespoons (2 fl oz/60 ml) olive oil, plus more for drizzling

Kosher salt and freshly ground pepper

6 plum (Roma) tomatoes, chopped

1½ lb (750 g) tail-on medium shrimp, peeled and deveined

½ cup (2½ oz/75 g) Kalamata olives, pitted

⅓ lb (155 g) feta cheese, crumbled

¼ cup (¼ oz/7 g) fresh oregano leaves

MEDITERRANEAN SHRIMP WITH FETA, OLIVES & OREGANO

Cook the Israeli couscous according to the package instructions. Stir in 2 tablespoons of the olive oil and season with salt and pepper. Cover to keep warm and set aside.

Preheat the oven to 400°F (200°C).

Lay the tomatoes in the bottom of a shallow 2-quart (2-l) baking dish and drizzle with the remaining 2 tablespoons olive oil. Bake just until the tomatoes release their juices, about 8 minutes. Remove from the oven and top with the shrimp, olives, feta, and oregano. Bake until the shrimp are bright pink and opaque throughout, 12–14 minutes.

Fill shallow bowls with couscous, top with the shrimp mixture, and drizzle with olive oil. Serve right away.

SERVES 4–6

PARTY FARE

-‹‹‹‹‹‹‹‹‹‹-

This colorful dish brims with Mediterranean flavors. To prepare as a party appetizer, use bay or smaller shrimp and serve with a sliced baguette. Shrimp is just as good and can be more economical purchased frozen rather than fresh. To defrost, place the frozen shrimp in the refrigerator for a few hours.

WHAT YOU NEED

Juice of 1½ lemons

1 tablespoon champagne vinegar

2 tablespoons chopped shallots

Kosher salt and freshly ground pepper

4 tablespoons olive oil

1 head radicchio, cored and torn into bite-sized pieces

1 bunch watercress, trimmed

¼ cup (⅓ oz/10 g) fresh parsley leaves, chopped

2 cans (15 oz/470 g each) Italian butter beans (lima beans), rinsed and drained

3 cans (15 oz/470 g each) best-quality olive oil–packed tuna

Gruyère toasts (see note) for serving

TUNA & BUTTER BEAN SALAD WITH RADICCHIO

PUT IT ON TOAST

Gruyère toasts are a great accompaniment to this salad. You may even want to pile salad on top of the toasts for a unique twist on a tuna melt. To make the toasts, preheat the broiler. Top four ¼-inch-thick (6-mm-thick) slices of crusty bread with 2 tablespoons of shredded Gruyère cheese. Slip under the broiler and broil until the cheese melts, 2–3 minutes.

In a small bowl, combine the lemon juice, vinegar, shallots, and salt and pepper to taste. Pour in the olive oil slowly, whisking until well blended. Taste and adjust the seasoning.

In a large bowl, combine the radicchio, watercress, and parsley. Add the beans and gently toss just to combine. Pour in the dressing and toss to coat all the ingredients well.

To assemble, divide the salad among 4 plates. Using a fork, place large chunks of tuna onto each plate. Serve right away, with the Gruyère toasts on the side.

SERVES 4

2 oranges

2½ tablespoons olive oil

2 teaspoons soy sauce

¾ teaspoon wasabi paste

1–2 ahi tuna steaks, 1 lb (500 g) total weight

⅓ cup (1 oz/30 g) black and/or white sesame seeds

3 heads Bibb lettuce, torn into bite-sized pieces

Citrus vinaigrette (see note)

2 ripe avocados, pitted, peeled, and sliced

SEARED TUNA & AVOCADO SALAD

Working over a bowl with 1 orange at a time and using a very sharp paring knife, pare away the peels and pith. Carefully cut between the membranes of the orange to release each orange section. Let the sections and juice fall into the bowl as you work.

In a bowl, stir together 1½ tablespoons of the olive oil, the soy sauce, and wasabi paste. Brush the tuna all over with the marinade. Spread the sesame seeds on a plate and press both sides of the tuna in the sesame seeds to coat.

Warm the remaining 1 tablespoon olive oil in a nonstick frying pan over high heat until very hot but not smoking. Add the tuna and cook, turning once, until golden brown but still rare inside, about 3 minutes per side. Transfer to a cutting board and cover loosely with aluminum foil.

Place the lettuce in a large salad bowl. Pour in the citrus vinaigrette to taste and toss to coat the lettuce well. Slice the tuna into ¼-inch (6-mm) slices.

Divide the lettuce among four plates. Arrange the tuna, avocado, and oranges on top and serve right away.

SERVES 4

DRESS YOUR GREENS

For a citrus vinaigrette to toss with the lettuce, in a small bowl, combine the juice of 2 limes, the juice of ½ an orange, 1 tablespoon rice vinegar, 1 teaspoon peeled and grated fresh ginger, 1 clove minced garlic, and salt and pepper to taste. Gradually whisk in 3 tablespoons olive oil until well blended. Taste and adjust the seasoning.

1 cup (7 oz/220 g) brown lentils

3 tablespoons red wine vinegar

2 tablespoons minced shallots

1½ tablespoons Dijon mustard

Kosher salt and freshly ground pepper

¼ cup (2 fl oz/60 ml) plus 2 teaspoons olive oil

1½ lb (750 g) center-cut wild salmon fillet, pin bones and skin removed, cut into 2 or 3 pieces

6 cups (6 oz/185 g) loosely packed baby arugula leaves

Lemon wedges for serving

SEARED SALMON & LENTILS WITH ARUGULA & VINAIGRETTE

COOKED TO PERFECTION

Ask your fishmonger for a center-cut fillet of salmon, which generally is the same thickness throughout, so it cooks evenly. Take care to not overcook the fish, and remember that it will continue to cook from residual heat once you pull it out of the oven. Salmon is best served when still pink at the center. Serve this dish with warm, crusty bread.

In a large, heavy-bottomed saucepan, add the lentils and 4 cups (32 fl oz/1 l) water. Bring the contents to a boil, reduce the heat to low, and simmer until tender, about 25 minutes. Drain and set aside.

In a small bowl, stir together the vinegar, shallots, mustard, and salt and pepper to taste. Pour in ¼ cup (2 fl oz/60 ml) of the olive oil slowly, whisking until well blended. Taste and adjust the seasoning.

Season the salmon with salt and pepper. Warm the remaining 2 teaspoons olive oil in a frying pan over high heat. Add the salmon and cook, turning once, until light pink throughout, 3–4 minutes per side. Transfer to a plate and let cool for 5 minutes. You can leave the salmon pieces intact or flake them into big 1½-inch (4-cm) chunks.

In another bowl, combine the arugula and lentils. Pour in three-fourths of the dressing and toss to coat all the ingredients well.

To assemble, mound the arugula and lentils on a platter and arrange the salmon on top. Drizzle the remaining dressing over the salmon and serve right away with lemon wedges.

SERVES 4

MAKE AHEAD

---

2 small skinless, boneless chicken breasts, about ¾ lb (375 g) total weight, or 1½ cups (9 oz/280 g) shredded rotisserie chicken

1 tablespoon olive oil

2 tablespoons chopped shallots

½ lb (250 g) fresh spinach leaves, tough stems removed

Kosher salt and freshly ground pepper

2 tablespoons heavy cream

All-purpose flour for rolling

2 sheets frozen puff pastry (one 17 oz/ 530 g package), thawed

1 large egg, lightly beaten

¼ lb (125 g) Gruyère cheese, shredded

Dijon mustard for serving

CHICKEN, SPINACH & GRUYÈRE TURNOVERS

If using chicken breasts, place them in a saucepan with cold water to cover by 1 inch (2.5 cm) and ½ teaspoon salt. Bring to a boil over high heat, reduce the heat to medium-low, and simmer until the chicken is opaque throughout, about 18 minutes. Drain and let cool. When cool enough to handle, shred the chicken. Set aside.

Preheat the oven to 400°F (200°C).

Warm the olive oil in a frying pan over medium-high heat. Add the shallots and sauté until soft, about 2 minutes. Add the spinach, season with salt and pepper, and sauté just until wilted, about 3 minutes. Stir in the heavy cream and cook just until combined, about 1 minute.

On a floured work surface, cut the puff pastry sheets in half to make 4 rectangles. Brush the edges with the egg. Pile the cooked chicken, the spinach, and cheese on half of each of the rectangles, leaving a ½-inch (12-mm) border. Fold the uncovered half of each rectangle over to cover the lower half. Crimp the edges with the tines of a fork. Using the tip of a sharp knife, cut a few small slits in the top of each turnover. Brush the tops with egg and place on a baking sheet lined with parchment paper. Bake until golden brown, 22–24 minutes. Let cool slightly and serve with mustard on the side.

SERVES 4

MAKE AHEAD

These savory turnovers can be assembled and frozen for up to 2 months. After crimping their edges, place them on a baking sheet in a single layer and freeze for at least 2 hours. Once frozen, stack the turnovers in a zippered plastic bag. To cook, brush the frozen turnovers with a beaten egg and bake for 25–28 minutes.

2 tablespoons olive oil, plus more for greasing

½ small yellow onion, chopped

2-inch (5-cm) piece of fresh ginger

2 cloves garlic, minced

2 tablespoons *each* ground cumin and ground coriander

½ teaspoon cinnamon

1 can (28 oz/875 g) crushed tomatoes

1 tablespoon firmly packed brown sugar

Kosher salt and freshly ground pepper

2 tablespoons fresh mint leaves, chopped

¼ cup (⅓ oz/10 g) fresh parsley leaves

1½ lb (750 g) ground lamb

1 large egg

½ teaspoon *each* garlic powder and dried oregano

1½ cups (9 oz/280 g) Israeli couscous

MOROCCAN LAMB MEATBALLS WITH SPICED TOMATO SAUCE

MAKE AHEAD

The tomato sauce can be refrigerated for up to 1 week or frozen for up to 1 month. Defrost frozen sauce in the refrigerator overnight and rewarm it in a saucepan over medium heat. The meatballs can be formed and refrigerated overnight or frozen for up to 1 month. To freeze, arrange them in a single layer on a baking sheet and place in the freezer for 2 hours. Transfer to a zippered plastic bag or an airtight container to store. Defrost overnight in the refrigerator and bake as instructed.

To make the tomato sauce, warm the olive oil in a saucepan over medium heat. Add the onion and sauté until translucent, about 5 minutes. Peel and grate the ginger. Add the minced ginger, the garlic, 1 tablespoon of the cumin, 1 tablespoon of the coriander, and ¼ teaspoon of the cinnamon and sauté just until the ginger and garlic are soft and the spices are toasted, about 2 minutes. Stir in the tomatoes with their juices and brown sugar. Raise the heat to medium-high and bring to a boil. Reduce the heat to low and simmer until the sauce darkens in color and thickens a bit, about 15 minutes. Season with salt and pepper to taste and stir in the mint. Reduce the heat to low and cover to keep warm.

Preheat the oven to 350°F (180°C). Chop the parsley. In a bowl, combine the lamb, parsley, egg, the remaining 1 tablespoon each cumin and coriander, the remaining ¼ teaspoon cinnamon, the garlic powder, and oregano. Using your hands, mix until roughly combined (do not overmix). Season well with salt and pepper. Form the lamb mixture into meatballs about the size of a golf ball, arranging them in a single layer on an oiled baking sheet as you work. Repeat until all the meat is used. Bake until cooked through, 15–18 minutes. While the meatballs are baking, cook the Israeli couscous according to the package directions. Cover to keep warm.

Spoon the couscous, tomato sauce, and meatballs into shallow bowls. Serve right away.

SERVES 4-6

WHAT YOU NEED

4 lb (2 kg) bone-in beef short ribs

Kosher salt and freshly ground pepper

3 tablespoons olive oil

2 carrots, chopped

2 ribs celery, chopped

1 yellow onion, chopped

5 fresh thyme sprigs

4 cloves garlic, minced

1 cup (8 fl oz/250 ml) red wine

4 cups (32 fl oz/1 l) low-sodium beef broth, plus more as needed

1 can (28 oz/875 g) chopped tomatoes

¼ cup (⅓ oz/10 g) fresh basil leaves, chopped

BRAISED SHORT RIB RAGÙ

MAKE AHEAD

The ragù can be refrigerated for up to 5 days or frozen for up to 1 month. If frozen, defrost it in the refrigerator overnight and rewarm in a saucepan over medium heat. This dish is delicious served over polenta. See page 18 for how to make polenta a day ahead of time.

Season the short ribs all over with salt and pepper and let stand at room temperature for 1 hour. Preheat the oven to 350°F (180°C). Warm 1 tablespoon of the olive oil in an ovenproof pot with a tight-fitting lid or a Dutch oven over medium-high heat. Working in batches as needed to avoid crowding, add the ribs to the pot and sear until browned on all sides, about 6 minutes total. Transfer to a plate and set aside.

Warm 1 tablespoon of the olive oil in the pot and add the carrots, celery, and half of the onion. Season with salt and pepper and sauté, stirring often, until the vegetables are very soft, about 7 minutes. Add the thyme and half of the garlic and sauté until the garlic is soft but not browned, about 2 minutes longer. Add the wine and, using a wooden spoon, scrape the bottom of the pan to deglaze the pot, and cook until it reduces by half, about 3 minutes. Pour in the broth and bring to a boil. Nestle the ribs in the liquid, cover the pot, and transfer to the oven. Bake until the meat falls off the bones, about 2½ hours. Every 45 minutes, check that the liquid reaches about three-fourths of the way up the sides of the ribs, adding more broth or water as needed.

Using tongs, transfer the ribs to a plate to cool. Set the pot with the cooking liquid aside to cool. When cool enough to handle, using your hands or 2 forks, shred the meat and set aside. Discard the bones. Strain the braising liquid and reserve 1 cup (8 fl oz/250 ml).

Warm the remaining 2 tablespoons olive oil in a frying pan over medium-high heat. Add the remaining onion and sauté until soft, about 5 minutes. Add the remaining garlic and sauté until the garlic is golden brown, about 1 minute. Add the tomatoes and their juices, the reserved braising liquid, and the shredded meat, season with salt and pepper, and cook until warmed through, 4–5 minutes. Stir in the basil and serve right away.

SERVES 4–6

WHAT YOU NEED

2 cups broccoli florets

All-purpose flour for dusting

1 lb (500 g) store-bought white or whole-wheat pizza dough

½ cup (4 fl oz/125 ml) tomato sauce

3 oz (90 g) salami, thinly sliced and cut into ¼-inch (6-mm) strips

1 cup (¼ lb/125 g) shredded provolone cheese

2 tablespoons freshly grated Parmesan cheese

Kosher salt and freshly ground pepper

1 large egg, lightly beaten

BROCCOLI, SALAMI & PROVOLONE STROMBOLI

Place a pizza stone in the oven and preheat to 450°F (230°C). Let the pizza stone heat at 450°F (230°C) for 15–30 minutes without opening the oven door.

Bring a pot of generously salted water to a boil over high heat. Add the broccoli and cook until bright green, about 3 minutes. Drain well in a colander, rinse under cold water, and drain again. Lay on top of paper towels to absorb any excess moisture. When cool enough to handle, chop into small pieces. Set aside.

On a floured pizza peel, stretch or roll out the pizza dough into a 10-by-14-inch (25-by-35-cm) rectangle. If the dough springs back, let it rest for about 10 minutes. With a long side facing you, spread the tomato sauce over the dough, leaving a 1-inch (2.5-cm) border on each short side and a 3-inch (7.5-cm) border on the long side across from you. Scatter the broccoli over the tomato sauce, then the salami, provolone, and Parmesan cheese. Season with salt and pepper.

Using a pastry brush, brush the egg on the uncovered edges of the dough. Fold over the 2 short sides to the 1-inch (2.5-cm) mark and brush the tops with the egg. With the short sides tucked in, tightly roll the stromboli lengthwise away from you. Crimp the seams tightly to seal. Turn the stromboli seam side down on the peel. Brush the stromboli all over with the egg. Using the tip of a sharp knife, make a few slits along the top of the dough, about 2 inches (5 cm) apart. Season lightly with salt and pepper.

Carefully slide the stromboli seam side down onto the hot stone in the oven. Bake until golden brown, 15–18 minutes. Using the peel, transfer the stromboli to a cutting board and let rest for 5 minutes. Carefully cut crosswise into slices and serve right away.

SERVES 4

MAKE AHEAD

A stromboli is really just a rolled pizza. To make ahead, assemble and freeze for up to 2 months. Brush with beaten egg and bake for 25–30 minutes at 450°F (230°C).

WHAT YOU NEED

10 tablespoons (6 fl oz/180 ml) olive oil

1½ tablespoons Worcestershire sauce

1½ tablespoons chopped fresh rosemary

1 large clove garlic, minced

Kosher salt and freshly ground pepper

1 lb (500 g) flank steak

5 tablespoons (3 fl oz/80 ml) balsamic vinegar

3 peaches, pitted and quartered

2 red onions, cut into ½-inch (12-mm) rings

2 tablespoons minced shallots

1 tablespoon Dijon mustard

2 heads red leaf or Bibb lettuce,
torn into bite-sized pieces

6 oz (185 g) crumbled blue cheese

FLANK STEAK & GRILLED PEACH SALAD WITH BLUE CHEESE

In a small bowl, whisk together 3 tablespoons of the olive oil, the Worcestershire sauce, rosemary, garlic, ½ teaspoon salt, and ¼ teaspoon pepper. Place the flank steak in a large zippered plastic bag and pour in the marinade. Let marinate in the refrigerator, turning the bag a few times, for at least 1 hour and up to overnight.

Meanwhile, build a medium-hot fire in a charcoal grill or preheat a gas grill to medium-high. Coat the grill grate lightly with cooking spray. Remove the steak from the marinade and let stand at room temperature for 20 minutes. (Discard the marinade.) Place the steak on the grate directly over the heat and grill, turning once, until grill-marked and cooked to the desired doneness, about 6 minutes per side for medium-rare. Transfer the steak to a cutting board, cover loosely with aluminum foil, and let rest for 10 minutes.

While the steak is resting, in a small bowl, whisk together 3 tablespoons of the olive oil and 2 tablespoons of the balsamic vinegar. Brush the peaches and onion all over and season lightly with salt and pepper. Arrange the peaches and onion directly over the heat and grill, turning once, until grill-marked, about 4 minutes per side. Transfer to a cutting board and let cool. Cut the peaches and the onions in half, then carve the steak against the grain on the diagonal into thin slices.

To make the dressing, in a small bowl, combine the remaining 3 tablespoons balsamic vinegar, the shallots, mustard, and salt and pepper to taste. Pour in the remaining 4 tablespoons (2 fl oz/60 ml) olive oil slowly, whisking until well blended. Place the lettuce in a large bowl and toss with dressing to taste. Mound the lettuce on a platter and top with the steak, peaches, onions, and blue cheese. Serve right away.

SERVES 6

MAKE AHEAD

The steak can be marinated for up to 24 hours. Bring it to room temperature for 20 minutes before grilling. The steak, onions, and peaches can be grilled 1 day in advance; let cool, then slice and store separately in zippered plastic bags in the refrigerator. The salad dressing can be covered and refrigerated for up to 1 week.

2 tablespoons canola oil

1 small yellow onion, chopped

1 poblano chile, seeded and chopped

2 cloves garlic, minced

1 tablespoon *each* chili powder and ground cumin

3 cans (15 oz/470 g each) black beans, rinsed and drained

1 can (14½ oz/455 g) chopped fire-roasted tomatoes

3 cups (24 fl oz/750 ml) low-sodium chicken or vegetable broth

1 cup (8 oz/250 g) quinoa

Kosher salt and freshly ground pepper

½ cup (¾ oz/20 g) fresh cilantro leaves, chopped

1 ripe avocado, pitted, peeled, and cubed

¾ cup (6 oz/185 g) Greek yogurt or sour cream

QUINOA & BLACK BEAN CHILI

MAKE AHEAD

The chili can be refrigerated for up to 5 days or frozen for up to 1 month. If frozen, defrost in the refrigerator overnight and rewarm in a saucepan over medium heat. If the quinoa has absorbed a lot of the liquid, add a bit more broth. Season with salt and pepper.

Warm the canola oil in a heavy-bottomed saucepan over medium heat. Add the onion and sauté until translucent, about 4 minutes. Add the poblano chile and sauté until soft, about 2 minutes. Add the garlic, chili powder, and cumin and sauté until the garlic is soft and the spices are toasted, about 1 minute.

Stir in the black beans, tomatoes with their juices, chicken broth, and quinoa. Raise the heat to medium-high and bring to a boil. Reduce the heat to medium-low and let simmer until the quinoa is tender, about 20 minutes. Season with salt and pepper to taste and stir in the cilantro. Ladle into bowls and top with the avocado and dollops of yogurt. Serve right away.

SERVES 6

WHAT YOU NEED

5 tablespoons (3 fl oz/80 ml) olive oil

1 yellow onion, finely chopped

2 cloves garlic, minced

1-inch (2.5-cm) piece of fresh ginger, peeled and grated

1 tablespoon ground cumin

2 teaspoons ground coriander

2 teaspoons ground turmeric

1 cinnamon stick

1 cup (7 oz/220 g) red lentils

2 tomatoes, chopped

4½ cups (36 fl oz/1.1 l) low-sodium chicken or vegetable broth

Kosher salt and freshly ground pepper

¼ cup (⅓ oz/10 g) fresh cilantro leaves, chopped

1 head cauliflower (about 2 lb/1 kg), thick stems removed, cut into small florets

INDIAN-SCENTED RED LENTILS WITH CAULIFLOWER "RICE"

Warm 2 tablespoons of the olive oil in a heavy-bottomed saucepan over medium heat. Add half of the onion and sauté until soft, about 4 minutes. Add the garlic, ginger, cumin, coriander, turmeric, and cinnamon and sauté just until the garlic and ginger are soft and the spices are toasted, about 2 minutes. Stir in the lentils, tomatoes, and 4 cups (32 fl oz/1 l) of the chicken broth. Raise the heat to medium-high and bring to a boil. Reduce the heat to medium-low and simmer until the lentils are soft and the mixture thickens, 25–30 minutes. Season well with salt and pepper and stir in the cilantro.

While the lentils cook, prepare the cauliflower "rice." Place the cauliflower florets into the bowl of a food processor and pulse until the cauliflower is uniformly finely chopped into the size of grains of rice, 30–40 pulses. Warm the remaining 3 tablespoons olive oil in a large frying pan. Add the remaining onion, season with salt and pepper, and sauté just until beginning to soften, about 3 minutes. Add the cauliflower, stir until all the "rice" is coated with oil, and sauté until soft, about 4 minutes. Add the remaining ½ cup (4 fl oz/125 ml) chicken broth and cook until the liquid is absorbed, about 3 minutes. Season well with salt and pepper.

Spoon the "rice" into shallow bowls and ladle lentils over the top. Serve right away.

SERVES 4–6

MAKE AHEAD

The lentils can be refrigerated for up to 5 days or frozen for up to 1 month. If frozen, defrost in the refrigerator overnight and rewarm in a saucepan over medium heat. The cauliflower "rice" can be refrigerated for up to 2 days. To rewarm, heat 1 or 2 tablespoons of olive oil in a frying pan over medium heat. Add the cauliflower and cook, stirring often, until warmed through.

2 cups (2 oz/60 g) stemmed fresh spinach

½ lb (250 g) fusilli pasta

½ lb (250 g) sweet Italian sausage

5 tablespoons freshly grated Parmesan cheese

Kosher salt and freshly ground pepper

2 tablespoons olive oil

½ small yellow onion, chopped

2 cloves garlic, minced

4 cups (32 fl oz/1 l) low-sodium chicken broth

1 can (14½ oz/455 g) diced fire-roasted tomatoes

2 tablespoons tomato paste

1 cup (½ lb/250 g) whole-milk ricotta

½ cup (2 oz/60 g) shredded mozzarella

6 fresh basil leaves, chopped

LASAGNA SOUP WITH RICOTTA & BASIL

MAKE AHEAD

The soup can be refrigerated for up to 2 days. Rewarm it in a saucepan over medium heat, adding more broth as needed. The meatballs can be formed and kept overnight in the refrigerator, or frozen for up to 1 month. To freeze, arrange them in a single layer on a baking sheet and place in the freezer for at least 2 hours then transfer to a zippered plastic bag. Defrost overnight in the refrigerator and bake as instructed. The ricotta topping can be covered and refrigerated for up to 4 days.

Preheat the oven to 375°F (190°C). Bring a large pot of generously salted water to a boil over high heat. Add the spinach and cook just until the leaves wilt, about 1 minute. Using a slotted spoon, transfer the spinach to a colander, drain well, and let cool on paper towels. Return the pot of water to a boil over high heat. Add the fusilli and cook according to the package directions. Drain well in a colander, rinse under cold water, and drain again. Transfer the pasta to a large bowl. Set aside.

Using the paper towels, wrap up the spinach and squeeze out all excess water. Chop the spinach and transfer to a bowl. Remove the sausage casings. Add the sausage and 2 tablespoons of the Parmesan cheese. Season with salt and pepper. Using your hands, mix together until combined. Form the sausage mixture into meatballs of about 1 teaspoon each, arranging them in a single layer on an oiled baking sheet as you work. Repeat until all the meatballs are formed. Bake until cooked through, 12–15 minutes. Set aside.

Warm the olive oil in a heavy-bottomed saucepan over medium heat. Add the onion and sauté until translucent, about 4 minutes. Add the garlic and sauté until softened, about 1 minute longer. Stir in the chicken broth, tomatoes with their juices, and tomato paste. Raise the heat to medium-high and bring to a boil. Reduce the heat to low and simmer until the broth thickens, about 15 minutes. Season with salt and pepper to taste. Add the meatballs and pasta and cook just until warmed through, about 2 minutes. In a small bowl, stir together the ricotta, mozzarella, and the remaining 3 tablespoons Parmesan cheese. Stir in the basil and season with pepper.

Ladle into shallow bowls and top with a generous dollop of the ricotta mixture. Serve right away.

SERVES 4–6

WHAT YOU NEED

6 poblano chiles

2 tablespoons olive oil

1 small yellow onion, chopped

1½ cups (280 g) fresh or thawed frozen
corn kernels

1 clove garlic, minced

1 teaspoon ground cumin

Kosher salt and freshly ground pepper

1 cup (5 oz/155 g) cooked white or brown rice

1 can (15 oz/470 g) black beans, rinsed
and drained

¼ cup (1/3 oz/10 g) fresh cilantro leaves,
chopped

½ cup (2 oz/60 g) plus 3 tablespoons shredded
Cheddar cheese

3 tablespoons sour cream or crème fraîche

STUFFED POBLANO CHILES

MAKE AHEAD

The stuffed and uncooked chiles
can be stored for up to 3 days
in the refrigerator. This is the
ultimate recipe for using up
leftovers because you can stuff
the poblanos with just about
anything. Try using couscous
or farro, and experiment with
different vegetables such as
tomatoes, bell peppers, summer
squash, and mushrooms. For
protein, add shredded chicken
or even ground beef.

Preheat the broiler. Place the poblanos on a baking sheet, slip under the broiler about
4 inches (10 cm) from the heat source, and broil, turning occasionally, until charred
black on all sides, about 8 minutes. Transfer the poblanos to a bowl, cover with plastic
wrap or a clean kitchen towel, and set aside to steam until slightly softened, about
5 minutes. When cool enough to handle, peel or rub away the charred skins, then cut a
2-inch (5-cm) slit lengthwise in each poblano. Using a small spoon, carefully scoop out
the seeds from the inside of each poblano and discard. Set the roasted poblanos aside.

Preheat the oven to 400°F (200°C).

Warm the olive oil in a frying pan over medium-high heat. Add the onion and cook,
stirring occasionally, until soft and translucent, about 5 minutes. Add the corn,
garlic, and cumin and stir to combine. Season with salt and pepper and cook, stirring
occasionally, just until the corn softens a bit, about 3 minutes. Transfer to a bowl and
stir in the rice, black beans, and cilantro. Add ½ cup of the cheese and the sour cream
and stir to combine. Season with salt and pepper.

Carefully spoon the rice mixture into the poblanos and place them in a 9-by-13-inch
(23-by-33-cm) baking dish. Top the stuffed poblanos with the remaining 3 tablespoons
of cheese. Add enough water to the baking dish so that it comes ½ inch (12 mm) up the
sides. Cover tightly with aluminum foil and bake until the filling is heated through and
the cheese is melted, about 20 minutes. Remove from the oven and, using a slotted
spoon, transfer the poblanos to a serving dish. Serve right away.

SERVES 4–6

1 lb (500 g) wild salmon fillet, pin bones and skin removed

⅓ cup (½ oz/15 g) panko bread crumbs

¼ cup (1¼ oz/35 g) finely chopped red onion

2 tablespoons chopped fresh dill

1 tablespoon Dijon mustard

1 large egg, lightly beaten

1 clove garlic, minced

Kosher salt and freshly ground pepper

½ cup (¼ lb/125 g) sour cream

Zest and juice of 1 lemon

1 tablespoon finely chopped fresh chives

2 teaspoons olive oil

DILLY SALMON CAKES WITH LEMONY SOUR CREAM

Finely chop the salmon and transfer to a large bowl. Add the panko, onion, dill, mustard, egg, and garlic. Using your hands, mix until roughly combined (do not overmix). Season generously with salt and pepper. Form the salmon mixture into 4 cakes and place them on a plate. Cover and refrigerate for at least 30 minutes or up to overnight.

In a small bowl, stir together the sour cream, lemon zest and juice, and the chives. Season with salt and pepper to taste.

Warm the olive oil in a nonstick frying pan over medium-high heat. Add the salmon cakes and cook until they are opaque throughout but not dried out, about 5 minutes per side. Serve right away, passing the lemony sour cream at the table.

SERVES 4

MAKE AHEAD

To freeze, stack the patties in an airtight container with parchment paper between them. Freeze for up to 1 month. Defrost the patties in the refrigerator overnight and cook according to the directions. The lemony sour cream can be refrigerated in an airtight container for up to 3 days.

1½ lb (750 g) center-cut wild salmon fillet, pin bones and skin removed, cut into 3 pieces

½ cup (4 fl oz/125 ml) white wine, plus more as needed

2 shallots, 1 sliced and 1 minced

8 black peppercorns

Kosher salt and freshly ground pepper

½ lb (250 g) fingerling potatoes, halved lengthwise

½ lb (250 g) haricots verts, trimmed

3 tablespoons fresh lemon juice

1 tablespoon Dijon mustard

5 tablespoons (3 fl oz/80 ml) olive oil

1 head romaine lettuce, torn into bite-sized pieces

6 hard-boiled eggs, peeled and quartered

4 Campari tomatoes, each cut into 8 wedges

½ cup (2½ oz/75 g) pitted Kalamata olives

POACHED SALMON NIÇOISE

In a deep, 10-inch (25-cm) frying pan with a tight-fitting lid, combine the salmon, white wine, ½ cup (4 fl oz/125 ml) water, the sliced shallot, peppercorns, and ½ teaspoon salt. Bring to a gentle boil over high heat, then reduce the heat to low, cover, and gently simmer until the salmon is light pink throughout, about 10 minutes. Using a large flat spatula, remove the salmon from the liquid and let cool. When cool enough to handle, cut the salmon into big chunks.

Place the potatoes in a heavy-bottomed saucepan with ½ teaspoon salt and add cold water to cover by 2 inches (5 cm). Bring to a boil over high heat, then reduce the heat to low and simmer until the potatoes are fork-tender, 6–8 minutes. Using tongs, remove the potatoes from the water and let cool. Return the saucepan of water to a boil over high heat. Add the haricots verts and cook for 2 minutes. Drain well in a colander, rinse under cold water, and drain again. Set aside.

In a bowl, combine the lemon juice, mustard, minced shallot, and salt and pepper to taste. Pour in the olive oil slowly, whisking until well blended. Taste and adjust the seasoning. Place the lettuce in another bowl. Pour in three-fourths of the dressing and toss to coat the lettuce well. Mound the lettuce in the middle of a platter and surround it with the salmon, eggs, potatoes, haricots verts, tomatoes, and olives. Drizzle with the remaining dressing and serve right away.

SERVES 4–6

MAKE AHEAD

The salad dressing and hard-boiled eggs can be prepared, covered, and refrigerated for up to 1 week in advance. The salmon, potatoes, and haricots verts can be cooked and refrigerated for up to 2 days. To prep salad greens 2–3 days in advance, wash the leaves and dry them well, tear them into bite-sized pieces, wrap tightly in paper towels (to absorb excess moisture), and place in a zippered plastic bag.

2 lemongrass stalks

2 tablespoons *each* soy sauce and canola oil

1½ tablespoons honey

2 teaspoons sesame oil

1-inch (2.5-cm) piece of fresh ginger, peeled and grated

1 clove garlic, minced

1½ lb (750 g) medium shrimp

½ cup (4 fl oz/125 ml) fresh lime juice

¼ cup (2 fl oz/60 ml) Asian fish sauce

1½ tablespoons firmly packed brown sugar

1 jalapeño chile, seeded and minced (optional)

½ head *each* green and red cabbage, shredded

2 cups (10 oz/315 g) shredded carrots

½ cup (¾ oz/20 g) fresh cilantro leaves

¼ cup (⅓ oz/10 g) fresh mint leaves

6–8 wooden skewers, soaked in water for at least 1 hour

¼ cup (1¼ oz/39 g) roasted peanuts, chopped

VIETNAMESE SLAW WITH LEMONGRASS SHRIMP & PEANUTS

MAKE AHEAD

The undressed slaw, dressing, and cooked shrimp skewers can be stored separately in zippered plastic bags or airtight containers and refrigerated 1 day in advance. Serve the shrimp and the slaw cold or at room temperature the next day.

Cut off the fattest, whitest part of the lemongrass stalk (about 3–4 inches/7.5–10 cm long). Unwrap the outer layer from the stalks and finely chop the smooth and shiny parts. In a large, nonreactive bowl, combine the lemongrass, soy sauce, canola oil, honey, sesame oil, ginger, and garlic. Peel and devein the shrimp. Add the shrimp to the bowl and toss to coat evenly. Cover and marinate in the refrigerator for at least 30 minutes and up to 2 hours.

In a small bowl, stir together the lime juice, fish sauce, brown sugar, and jalapeño, if using. In a large salad bowl, toss together the cabbages, carrots, cilantro, and mint. Pour in the dressing and toss to coat all the ingredients well. Let stand at room temperature, stirring a few times, while you cook the shrimp.

Remove the shrimp from the refrigerator and thread 3–5 shrimp onto each skewer. Warm a grill pan or frying pan over high heat. Coat with nonstick cooking spray and add the shrimp. Cook until bright pink and opaque throughout, about 3 minutes per side.

Mound the slaw on a platter, top with the skewers, and sprinkle with the peanuts. Serve right away.

SERVES 4

SHEET PAN DINNERS

WHAT YOU NEED

4 firm whitefish fillets, such as cod, sea bass, or haddock, about 6 oz (185 g) each

Kosher salt and freshly ground pepper

1 cup (14½ oz/455 g) canned diced tomatoes

1 cup (5 oz/155 g) Niçoise olives, pitted

⅓ cup (2½ oz/75 g) capers, drained

1 cup (1 oz/30 g) fresh basil leaves, chopped

8 fresh thyme sprigs

4 small zucchini, cut into ¼-inch (6-mm) rounds

3 tablespoons olive oil

FISH PUTTANESCA EN PAPILLOTE WITH ZUCCHINI

PERFECT LITTLE PACKETS

>>>>>>>>>>

En papillote refers to food baked in parchment-paper bundles. The parchment creates a pocket of steam, so food stays moist. This method of cooking makes cleanup a breeze and is also very healthy because it requires hardly any butter or oil. Plus, it's a fun treat to let diners open their own packet. (Take care when opening the packets, as they will be filled with steam.) You can place the packets right onto plates, or serve the fish atop a grain, such as rice pilaf or farro, to soak up the delicious juices.

Preheat the oven to 350°F (180°C).

Cut parchment paper into four 9-inch (23-cm) squares and place on a baking sheet. Arrange each piece of fish in the middle of each square. Season each piece with salt and pepper and distribute the tomatoes with their juices, olives, capers, basil, and thyme evenly among the packets. Season again with salt and pepper.

To close the packets, gather together 2 sides of the parchment paper and fold the edges over. Tuck the remaining 2 sides of the parchment paper under the fish. (Do not seal the packet too tightly because enough air needs to circulate to steam the fish. The seal should just be enough so that steam doesn't escape.) Repeat to make 3 more packets.

Pile the zucchini onto the baking sheet next to the packets. Drizzle with the olive oil, season well with salt and pepper, and toss to coat. Spread the zucchini in a single layer.

Bake until the zucchini is fork-tender and the flesh of the fish is opaque throughout and flakes easily with a fork, about 20 minutes.

Carefully open the packets and transfer the fish and zucchini to plates or place a packet on each plate and have diners open their own packets. Serve right away.

SERVES 4

1 big bunch broccoli rabe, tough stems removed

4 tablespoons (2 fl oz/60 ml) olive oil

Kosher salt and freshly ground pepper

1½ lb (750 g) tail-on medium shrimp, peeled and deveined

2 teaspoons Dijon mustard

2 cloves garlic, minced

½ lemon

LEMONY SHRIMP & BROCCOLI RABE

Preheat the oven to 400°F (200°C).

Pile the broccoli rabe on a baking sheet lined with parchment paper. Drizzle with 2 tablespoons of the olive oil, season well with salt and pepper, and toss to coat. Spread the broccoli rabe in a single layer on half of the baking sheet. Bake for 8 minutes.

While the broccoli rabe is cooking, in a large bowl, combine the shrimp with the remaining 2 tablespoons olive oil, the mustard, and garlic. Season well with salt and pepper and toss to coat evenly. Transfer the shrimp to a sheet of aluminum foil and spread in a single layer. Fold the edges of the foil up into a "bowl" so that the cooking juices don't spill over.

Once the broccoli rabe has cooked for 8 minutes, transfer the shrimp with the foil to the prepared baking sheet and place next to the broccoli rabe. Roast until the shrimp are bright pink and opaque throughout and the broccoli rabe stems are fork-tender, 8–10 minutes. Remove from the oven and squeeze the lemon juice all over the shrimp and broccoli rabe. Serve right away.

SERVES 4

DINNER IN A FLASH

You will barely have time to set the table before this dinner is ready to devour—the shrimp and the broccoli rabe cook on the same baking sheet. Leaving their tails on will keep the shrimp from curling up into tiny balls during cooking. Orzo pasta tossed with olive oil and Parmesan cheese is an easy accompaniment to round out the meal.

3 tablespoons low-sodium soy sauce

3 tablespoons sake

3 tablespoons white miso paste

2 tablespoons mirin

1½ tablespoons firmly packed
golden brown sugar

4 center-cut wild salmon steaks, about 6 oz
(185 g) each, pin bones and skin removed

5 bok choy, about 1 lb (500 g) total weight,
quartered

2 tablespoons olive oil

Kosher salt and freshly ground pepper

2 tablespoons chopped fresh chives

2 tablespoons fresh lemon juice

ASIAN-GLAZED SALMON WITH BOK CHOY

ALL ABOUT MISO

Miso is a wonderful condiment to keep in the refrigerator—it's high in health benefits due to its fermentation, it keeps for a long time, and it adds salty umami flavor to fish, meat, vegetables, and even salad dressings. You can make miso soup by whisking miso to taste into boiling water. Red miso is a bit stronger than white, while white miso has a more mellow taste; both will work in this recipe.

In a small bowl, whisk together the soy sauce, sake, miso paste, mirin, and brown sugar. Set ¼ cup (2 fl oz/60 ml) of the marinade aside. Place the salmon on a plate and pour the remaining marinade over the top. Cover and let marinate in the refrigerator for at least 30 minutes and up to 8 hours.

Preheat the oven to 400°F (200°C). Coat a baking sheet with cooking spray.

Remove the salmon from the marinade and place it on the baking sheet. Pile the bok choy onto the baking sheet next to the salmon. Drizzle with the olive oil, season well with salt and pepper, and toss to coat. Spread the bok choy into a single layer. Bake until the bok choy are fork-tender and the flesh of the fish is opaque throughout and flakes easily with a fork, about 15 minutes. Remove from the oven and spoon the reserved marinade over the salmon, followed by the chives. Sprinkle the lemon juice all over the bok choy. Serve right away.

SERVES 4

WHAT YOU NEED

3 skinless, boneless chicken breasts, about 1 lb (500 g) total weight

¾ cup (6 fl oz/180 ml) plus 2 tablespoons olive oil

Kosher salt and freshly ground pepper

6 assorted beets, about 4 lb (2 kg) total weight, trimmed, peeled, and quartered

3 shallots, unpeeled, trimmed, and halved

1 large clove garlic, unpeeled

2 tablespoons balsamic vinegar

1½ teaspoons Dijon mustard

10 cups (10 oz/315 g) mixed greens

¼ cup (⅓ oz/10 g) fresh tarragon leaves

1 apple, cored and chopped

¼ cup (1¼ oz/35 g) slivered blanched almonds, toasted

ROASTED CHICKEN WITH BEETS, GREENS & APPLES

Preheat the oven to 375°F (190°C).

Place the chicken breasts on one half of a baking sheet lined with aluminum foil. Drizzle with 1 tablespoon of the olive oil, season with salt and pepper, and toss to coat. Place the beets, shallots, and garlic on a piece of aluminum foil and drizzle with the remaining 1 tablespoon olive oil. Wrap loosely in the foil and place on the baking sheet. Roast until the chicken is opaque throughout, about 25 minutes. Transfer the chicken to a cutting board to cool and return the baking sheet to the oven. Continue roasting until the beets are fork-tender and the shallots are very soft, about 45 minutes. Remove from the oven and let cool.

When cool enough to handle, shred the chicken and set aside.

To make the vinaigrette, combine the balsamic vinegar and mustard in a blender. Squeeze in the roasted garlic and add the shallots, discarding the skins. Blend until well combined, about 20 seconds. Put the ¾ cup (6 fl oz/180 ml) olive oil in a measuring cup with a spout. With the blender running, add the olive oil from the measuring cup in a steady stream. Blend until the dressing is emulsified. Season with salt and pepper to taste. (Leftover dressing can be refrigerated for up to 2 weeks.)

In a large bowl, toss the mixed greens and tarragon. Pour in the dressing to taste and toss to coat all the ingredients. Mound the greens on a platter and arrange the chicken, beets, apple, and almonds on top. Serve right away.

SERVES 4

HOMEMADE DRESSING

Homemade salad dressings are worth every minute of effort, and they are healthier because you can control the quality and quantity of the ingredients. Most salad dressings, including this one, will keep in an airtight container in the refrigerator for up to 2 weeks. A mason jar with a tight-fitting lid is a great way to store dressings; you can simply shake the jar to combine the ingredients.

¾ cup (6 oz/185 g) plain whole-milk yogurt

1 teaspoon *each* ground cumin and turmeric

½ teaspoon *each* smoked paprika, saffron threads, and ground cinnamon

Kosher salt and freshly ground pepper

1½ lb (750 g) skinless, boneless chicken breasts

1½ lb (750 g) asparagus, tough woody ends trimmed

2 tablespoons olive oil

2 preserved lemons, drained, preserving liquid reserved

8–10 wooden skewers (7 inches/18 cm or longer), soaked in water for at least 1 hour

YOGURT-SPICED CHICKEN & PRESERVED LEMON SKEWERS

LEMON POWER

>>>>>>>>>>

If you can't find preserved lemons in the speciality foods aisle of your grocery store and don't have time to make your own, simply roast slices of raw lemons. Remember to always wash the outside of lemon with warm soapy water if you plan to eat the peel. Turmeric bursts with health-boosting properties, but use it carefully—it will stain absorbent surfaces.

In a large, nonreactive bowl, stir together the yogurt, cumin, turmeric, paprika, saffron, cinnamon, ½ teaspoon salt, and ¼ teaspoon pepper.

Cut the chicken into 1½-inch (4-cm) cubes. Add the chicken to the bowl and toss to coat well. Cover and let marinate in the refrigerator for at least 1 hour or up to 24 hours.

Preheat the oven to 375°F (190°C). Line a baking sheet with aluminum foil.

In a large bowl, toss the asparagus with the olive oil and the reserved preserved lemon liquid (about 1 tablespoon). Set aside. Cut the lemons into 1-inch (2.5-cm) pieces.

Drain the skewers and thread them with chicken and lemons. Place the skewers in a single layer on half of the baking sheet. Bake until the chicken is opaque throughout, about 15 minutes. Using tongs, flip the skewers over. Spread the asparagus in a single layer next to the skewers on the baking sheet. Cook until the chicken is roasted throughout and the asparagus is fork-tender, about 12 minutes. Serve right away.

SERVES 4

5 tablespoons (3 fl oz/80 ml) olive oil

½ small yellow onion, chopped

2 cloves garlic, minced

1 tablespoon Worcestershire sauce

1 lb (500 g) ground beef

1 lb (500 g) ground pork

¼ cup (½ oz/15 g) fresh bread crumbs

1 large egg, lightly beaten

Kosher salt and freshly ground pepper

½ cup (4 oz/125 g) tomato ketchup

4 carrots, peeled and cut
into ⅓-inch (9-mm) pieces

3 parsnips, peeled and cut
into ⅓-inch (9-mm) pieces

2 teaspoons chopped fresh rosemary

CLASSIC MEAT LOAF WITH ROSEMARY-ROASTED VEGETABLES

Preheat the oven to 375°F (190°C). Line a baking sheet with aluminum foil.

Warm 2 tablespoons of the olive oil in a frying pan over medium-high heat. Add the onion and sauté until translucent, about 4 minutes. Add the garlic and sauté until softened, about 1 minute longer. Stir in the Worcestershire sauce, remove from the heat, and let cool.

In a bowl, combine the beef, pork, the onion mixture, the bread crumbs, egg, 1 teaspoon salt, and ½ teaspoon pepper. Using your hands, mix until thoroughly combined. Divide the meat in half and, using your hands again, form two identical loaves, each about 10 inches (25 cm) long and 4 inches (10 cm) wide. Place the loaves on half of the baking sheet and spread the ketchup on top.

Pile the carrots and parsnips onto the baking sheet next to the meat loaves. Drizzle with the remaining 3 tablespoons olive oil and the rosemary, season well with salt and pepper, and toss to coat. Spread the carrots and parsnips into a single layer. Bake, stirring the vegetables once about halfway through, until the vegetables are caramelized on the edges and fork-tender and an instant-read thermometer inserted into the meat loaves reaches 145°F (63°C), about 45 minutes. Remove the baking sheet from the oven and transfer the meat loaves to a cutting board. Cut the meat loaves into thick slices and serve with the vegetables.

SERVES 4-6

FREE-FORM DINNER

Here, we've eliminated the use of loaf pans by free-forming two meat loaves right on the baking sheet, alongside a hearty and colorful medley of root vegetables. While this recipe calls for equal parts beef and pork, you can experiment with any combination of ground meats, including lamb, veal, and turkey. Leftover meatloaf makes fabulous sandwiches.

1½ lb (750 g) brussels sprouts, halved

3 tablespoons olive oil

1 tablespoon balsamic vinegar

Kosher salt and freshly ground pepper

6 fresh thyme sprigs

6 assorted sausages, such as Italian, chicken apple, and/or bratwurst

1 baguette, thinly sliced or cut into 4–6 lengths

Spicy mustard for serving

SAUSAGE & BRUSSELS SPROUTS BAKE WITH SPICY MUSTARD

QUICK FIX

Requiring only a few fresh ingredients and taking 45 minutes or less, this inexpensive and super-satisfying meal is ideal for a busy weeknight supper. Choose any type of sausage you like, or use a variety. Buy fresh uncooked sausages, usually found at the butcher's counter, for this recipe. You can substitute sliced onions and peppers for the brussels sprouts and serve with hoagie rolls.

Preheat the oven to 450°F (230°C). Line a baking sheet with aluminum foil.

Pile the brussels sprouts on the baking sheet. Drizzle with the olive oil and balsamic vinegar, season well with salt and pepper, and toss to coat. Spread the brussels sprouts in a single layer and lay the thyme sprigs on top. Bake for 10 minutes.

Remove the brussels sprouts from the oven, toss them once, and move them to one side of the baking sheet. Spread the sausages in a single layer on the other side of the baking sheet. Bake, flipping the sausages about halfway through, until the sausages are cooked through and the brussels sprouts are caramelized, 20–25 minutes. Serve, passing the baguette and mustard at the table, and encourage diners to make small baguette sandwiches with the mustard, brussels sprouts, and sausages.

SERVES 4–6

WHAT YOU NEED

1 boneless beef eye-round roast, about 2½ lb (1.25 kg), preferably with a layer of fat

8 cloves garlic

4 tablespoons (2 fl oz/60 ml) olive oil

Kosher salt and freshly ground pepper

1½ lb (750 g) Yukon gold potatoes, scrubbed

2 tablespoons chopped fresh parsley

HORSERADISH SAUCE

1¼ cups (10 fl oz/310 ml) mayonnaise

2 tablespoons prepared horseradish

1 tablespoon Dijon mustard

1 tablespoon fresh lemon juice

Kosher salt and freshly ground pepper

ROAST BEEF WITH SMASHED POTATOES & HORSERADISH SAUCE

Let the beef stand at room temperature for about 1 hour.

Preheat the oven 400°F (200°C). Line a baking sheet with aluminum foil.

Using the tip of a small sharp knife, make 8 slits in the beef and insert a garlic clove into each slit. Brush the beef with 2 tablespoons of the olive oil and season all over with salt and pepper. Place the beef on half of the baking sheet.

In a large bowl, combine the potatoes and the remaining 2 tablespoons olive oil. Season well with salt and pepper and toss to coat. Spread the potatoes in a single layer next to the beef on the baking sheet. Bake until the potatoes are fork-tender and an instant-read thermometer inserted into the thickest part of the beef reaches 130°F (54°C), 40–50 minutes.

While the beef and potatoes cook, make the horseradish sauce. In a small bowl, stir together the mayonnaise, horseradish, mustard, and lemon juice. Season with salt and pepper to taste and set aside.

Remove the beef and potatoes from the oven, cover loosely with aluminum foil, and let the beef rest for 10 minutes. Using a potato masher or large fork, lightly crush each potato until it splits open and sprinkle the parsley on top. Carve the beef into thin ¼-inch (6-mm) slices. Serve right away, passing the horseradish sauce at the table.

SERVES 6

QUICK-FIX ROAST

A classic roast of juicy beef and tender potatoes is usually reserved for Sunday, but this simpler version is on the table in about 1 hour. The layer of fat on the beef is important: it adds flavor and will keep the roast moist during cooking. You'll want to dress your entire meal in the tangy, slightly spicy, horseradish sauce.

1 pork tenderloin, about 1½ lb (750 g)

3 tablespoons olive oil

Kosher salt and freshly ground pepper

14 fresh sage leaves

5 thin slices prosciutto, each
about 4 inches (10 cm) wide

1 head cauliflower, thick stems removed,
cut into florets

½ teaspoon paprika

¼ teaspoon ground cinnamon

PROSCIUTTO & SAGE-WRAPPED PORK WITH CAULIFLOWER

ROASTED TO PERFECTION

Roasting vegetables on parchment paper keeps them from sticking to the baking sheet and allows them to brown beautifully. Do yourself a favor and cook two pork tenderloins; leftover slices of pork make wonderful sandwiches on a baguette with Dijon mustard.

Preheat the oven to 400°F (200°C). Line a baking sheet with parchment paper.

Brush the tenderloin with 1 tablespoon of the olive oil and season all over with salt and pepper. Lay 10 sage leaves crosswise on top of the tenderloin and then wrap the prosciutto around the roast, overlapping as needed. Brush the prosciutto all over with ½ tablespoon of the olive oil and lay the remaining 4 sage leaves crosswise on top. Transfer the tenderloin, seam side down, to a sheet of aluminum foil. Fold the edges of the foil up into a "bowl" so that the cooking juices don't spill over.

In a bowl, toss the cauliflower with the remaining 1½ tablespoons olive oil, ¾ teaspoon salt, the paprika, cinnamon, and ¼ teaspoon pepper. Spread the cauliflower in a single layer on the baking sheet, leaving space for the tenderloin. Bake the cauliflower for 20 minutes, remove the baking sheet from the oven, stir the cauliflower, transfer the tenderloin with the foil to the baking sheet, and return the baking sheet to the oven. Bake until the cauliflower is golden brown and fork-tender and an instant-read thermometer inserted into the thickest part of the tenderloin reaches 145°F (63°C), about 20 minutes.

Remove from the oven and let the tenderloin rest for 10 minutes. Carve into thick ½-inch (12-mm) slices. Serve right away with the cauliflower.

SERVES 4

WHAT YOU NEED

1 lb (500 g) extra-firm tofu, drained

⅓ cup (3 fl oz/80 ml) low-sodium soy sauce

3 tablespoons dark sesame oil

2 tablespoons rice vinegar or sherry vinegar

3-inch (7.5-cm) piece of fresh ginger, peeled and grated

2 cloves garlic, minced

¾ lb (375 g) green beans, trimmed

½ lb (250 g) shiitake mushrooms, brushed clean and halved

PEANUT SAUCE

6 tablespoons (3¾ oz/115 g) peanut butter

2 tablespoons soy sauce

4 teaspoons sesame oil

4 teaspoons rice vinegar

¼ cup (2 fl oz/60 ml) hot water

BAKED TOFU WITH GREEN BEANS, SHIITAKES & PEANUT SAUCE

Place 3 paper towels on a plate and lay the tofu on the towels. Top with 3 more paper towels and another plate. Use something heavy, such as a pot, to add weight to the top plate. Let stand for 5 minutes. Change the paper towels and repeat the process once more. This will remove excess moisture from the tofu so that it will caramelize with the marinade. Cut the tofu into ¾-inch (2-cm) cubes.

In a large bowl, stir together the soy sauce, sesame oil, vinegar, ginger, and garlic. Add the tofu, green beans, and mushrooms and toss to coat all the ingredients well. Let marinate at room temperature for 30 minutes, tossing a few times.

Preheat the oven to 400°F (200°C). Line a baking sheet with aluminum foil. Spread the tofu, green beans, and mushrooms in a single layer and roast, stirring once about halfway through, until the tofu is caramelized on the edges and the vegetables are fork-tender, about 30 minutes.

While the tofu and vegetables are cooking, make the peanut sauce. In a bowl, combine the peanut butter, soy sauce, sesame oil, and vinegar. Stir in the hot water until smooth and creamy.

Divide the tofu and vegetables among 4 plates and serve, passing the peanut sauce at the table.

SERVES 4

EASY AS CAN BE

Here's a simple "stir-fry" that bakes in the oven, making cleanup a snap. Adults and children alike will love this creamy peanut sauce, and making it is as easy as stirring together a few ingredients; no stove top or blender needed. Serve this dish over brown rice or toss it with udon noodles.

12 lamb rib or loin chops, ¾ inch (2 cm) thick, about 2½ lb (1.25 kg) total

5 tablespoons (3 fl oz/80 ml) olive oil

Zest and juice of 1 lemon

Kosher salt and freshly ground pepper

1 acorn squash, about 1½ lb (750 g), halved, seeded, and cut into ½-in (12-mm) slices

FETA-POMEGRANATE TOPPING

2 oz (60 g) feta cheese, crumbled

⅓ cup (⅓ oz/10 g) fresh parsley leaves, chopped

⅓ cup (1½ oz/45 g) pomegranate seeds

Zest of 1 lemon

1 teaspoon olive oil

LAMB CHOPS WITH FETA-POMEGRANATE TOPPING & SQUASH

FIT FOR COMPANY

>>>>>>>>>>>

This dish is simple enough for a weeknight dinner but impressive enough for weekend company. Lamb chops cook quickly in the oven and are filled with naturally delicious flavor. When pomegranates are out of season, they can be replaced with dried cranberries. Pair this meal with a simple arugula salad and red wine or cranberry spritzers.

Preheat the oven to 375°F (190°C). Line a baking sheet with aluminum foil.

In a large bowl, combine the lamb chops with 3 tablespoons of the olive oil and the lemon zest and juice. Season well with salt and pepper and toss to coat evenly. Let the lamb stand at room temperature for about 15 minutes.

Pile the squash on the baking sheet. Drizzle with the remaining 2 tablespoons olive oil, season well with salt and pepper, and toss to coat. Spread the squash in a single layer and bake, about 10 minutes.

Remove the squash from the oven and add the lamb chops all over the baking sheet. Bake until the squash is fork-tender and caramelized around the edges and an instant-read thermometer inserted into the thickest part of a lamb chop reaches 130°F (54°C), about 20 minutes. (Do not flip the lamb chops.)

While the lamb cooks, make the topping. In a small bowl, stir together the feta, parsley, pomegranate seeds, lemon zest, and olive oil. Season with salt and pepper and set aside.

Remove the lamb from the oven, cover loosely with aluminum foil, and let rest for 10 minutes. Place the lamb and squash on a platter and sprinkle with the topping. Serve right away.

SERVES 4

SIMPLE DESSERTS

3 firm but ripe pears, such as Bosc

2 tablespoons unsalted butter,
at room temperature

¾ teaspoon ground cinnamon

½ teaspoon pure vanilla extract

¾ cup (6 fl oz/180 ml) apple juice or cider,
plus more as needed

½ cup (5 oz/155 g) purchased caramel sauce,
warmed

BAKED CINNAMON PEARS WITH CARAMEL SAUCE

PERFECT PEARS

Pop this dessert in the oven right before your family sits down to dinner, and it'll be ready just in time for dessert. When choosing pears, pick ones that are ripe but still firm. In lieu of caramel sauce, try this with whipped cream or chocolate syrup. This is already a relatively healthy treat, but you can up the nutrition by serving it with Greek yogurt and granola.

Preheat the oven to 350°F (180°C).

Cut the pears in half lengthwise, keeping the stem intact, and core.

In a small bowl, stir together the butter, cinnamon, and vanilla. Using your hands or a pastry brush, rub the butter mixture all over the pears. Place the pears, cut side down, in a 9-by-13-inch (23-by-33-cm) baking dish. Pour the apple juice around the pears.

Bake the pears for 30 minutes. Remove from the oven, flip the pears, and add more apple juice as needed. Continue baking until the pears are soft when pierced with the tip of a sharp knife, about 30 minutes longer.

Transfer the pears to a platter and drizzle with caramel sauce. Serve right away.

SERVES 4–6

¾ cup (6 oz/185 g) mascarpone cheese, at room temperature

Zest and juice of 1 small orange

Six ½-inch (12-mm) slices challah, brioche, or baguette

1 cup (¼ lb/125 g) blueberries

Honey for drizzling

ORANGE-MASCARPONE TOASTS WITH BLUEBERRIES & HONEY

In a small bowl, stir together the mascarpone and the orange zest and juice. Set aside.

Lightly toast the bread slices in a toaster. Let cool slightly. Generously spread each bread slice with the mascarpone mixture and top with blueberries. Drizzle with honey and serve right away.

SERVES 4–6

JUST SWEET ENOUGH

Mascarpone is a sweet, soft cheese similar to cream cheese. This dessert straddles the border between sweet and savory, which makes it a nice midweek treat. Serve it after a light meal, such as roasted chicken (page 93) or baked eggs (page 42). Try the orange-mascarpone stuffed into pitted dates for a delicious after-school snack.

2 apples, such as Granny Smith

2 tablespoons sugar

½ teaspoon pumpkin pie spice

9 sheets filo dough, thawed if frozen

3 tablespoons unsalted butter, melted

⅓ cup (3 oz/90 g) apple or apricot jelly, warmed

APPLE FILO TART

SWEET TREAT

Store-bought filo makes a buttery and flaky base for any tart, savory or sweet. In place of apples, you can use fresh pears, figs, or berries. To make individual tarts, cut the assembled tart into squares before baking. A scoop of vanilla ice cream is, of course, an excellent way to top off a warm apple tart.

Preheat the oven to 350°F (180°C).

Peel, core, and thinly slice the apples. In a bowl, combine the apples, sugar, and pumpkin pie spice and toss to coat evenly. Set aside.

Line a baking sheet with parchment paper. Place 1 sheet of filo dough onto the baking sheet and brush all over with melted butter. Top with 2 more sheets of filo dough and brush all over with melted butter. Repeat with the remaining filo dough and melted butter.

Leaving a 1-inch (2.5-cm) border around the edges, arrange the apple slices in overlapping rows. Fold the uncovered sides of the filo dough over so that they cover just about ¼ inch (6 mm) of the apples. Press down to create a border. Brush the tart all over with the jelly. Bake until the tart is golden brown, about 20 minutes. Let cool slightly, slice into squares, and serve right away.

SERVES 4-6

¾ cup (6 oz/185 g) sugar

1 cup (8 fl oz/250 ml) fresh lemon juice

4 fresh thyme sprigs

LEMON-THYME GRANITA

In a saucepan over medium heat, combine 2 cups (16 fl oz/500 ml) water and the sugar. Bring the mixture to a simmer, and cook, stirring occasionally, until the sugar dissolves, 2–3 minutes. Turn off the heat and add the thyme sprigs. Let stand for 30 minutes.

Strain the liquid through a fine-mesh sieve, discarding the thyme. Stir in the lemon juice and transfer to a 9-by-13-inch (23-by-33-cm) glass baking dish. Freeze until crystals just begin to form, about 30 minutes. Using the tines of a fork, scrape to break up the frozen bits every 30 minutes for 3–4 hours, until the mixture resembles shaved ice.

Spoon into bowls and serve right away or cover and freeze for up to 1 week.

SERVES 6

KIDS CAN MAKE IT

This is a fun dessert for kids to make themselves. It's perfect for an after-school activity, and you can use the intermittent scraping as an opportunity for a quick homework break. Try other citrus fruits here, including limes and blood oranges, and omit the thyme if you prefer. Serve the granita in wineglasses for a celebratory night, or in paper cups, like shaved ice at the boardwalk.

2 large stalks rhubarb, about 1 lb (500 g), cut into ½-inch (12-mm) pieces

1 cup (4 oz/125 g) raspberries

⅓ cup (3 oz/90 g) sugar

1 quart (28 oz/880 g) vanilla ice cream

FRESH RHUBARB-RASPBERRY SAUCE WITH ICE CREAM

GOOD ON EVERYTHING

→ »»»»»»»»»

Ready to serve in under 15 minutes, this tangy sauce is great with vanilla ice cream, and one you can feel good about since rhubarb is actually a vegetable. Use the sauce to top pound cake, or even pancakes for a weekend breakfast. Discard the leaves on the rhubarb stalks, as they are inedible and poisonous.

In a heavy-bottomed saucepan over medium heat, combine the rhubarb, raspberries, sugar, and ¼ cup (2 fl oz/60 ml) water. Cook, stirring occasionally, until the rhubarb is soft, about 10 minutes. Set aside and let cool slightly.

Scoop the vanilla ice cream into dishes and top with the rhubarb-raspberry sauce. Serve right away.

SERVES 4–6

½ cup (2 oz/125 g) sugar

¼ cup (¾ oz/20 g) unsweetened cocoa powder

2 tablespoons cornstarch

½ teaspoon kosher salt

2 cups (16 fl oz/500 ml) whole milk

1 tablespoon unsalted butter

1 teaspoon pure vanilla extract

1 pint (½ lb/250 g) strawberries, with stems

HOMEMADE CHOCOLATE PUDDING WITH STRAWBERRY DIPPERS

In a heavy-bottomed saucepan, whisk together the sugar, cocoa powder, cornstarch, and salt. Add the milk, whisking to combine, and set the pan over medium heat. Bring to a boil, stirring constantly with a wooden spoon, and cook until the pudding thickens, 2–3 minutes. Turn off the heat and stir in the butter and vanilla.

Ladle the pudding into four 4-oz (125-g) ramekins or small bowls and let cool.

Serve warm, at room temperature, or chilled, passing the strawberries at the table for dipping.

SERVES 4

KEEP IT SIMPLE

Sometimes, classics are best and just what is needed to get through a busy week. These strawberry dippers are fun for kids and are a terrific pairing with the rich chocolate pudding, as is a dollop of fresh whipped cream. The pudding can be made up to 3 days ahead and stored in an airtight container in the refrigerator.

3 tablespoons unsalted butter, at room temperature

8 slices bread, such as whole wheat, baguette, or sourdough

¾ cup (7½ oz/235 g) Nutella spread

1 cup (1¾ oz/50 g) mini marshmallows

NUTELLA & MINI MARSHMALLOW PANINI

MIRACLE SANDWICH

>>>>>>>>>

Make this dessert sandwich, and your kids will sing your praises for days! Try substituting sliced strawberries, bananas, or even ripe pear for the marshmallows. If you don't have any bread lying around, 2 frozen waffles will do the trick. This also makes an indulgent Sunday brunch dish. Let the panini rest for a minute before serving, as the chocolate will be very hot.

Preheat a panini maker or heat a grill pan or a large frying pan over medium heat.

Spread one side of each bread slice with the butter. Lay the bread slices, buttered sides down, on a work surface. Spread the Nutella on 4 of the slices and top with the marshmallows. Cover with the remaining bread slices, buttered sides up.

Place the sandwiches in the panini maker, 2 at a time, and close the lid. If you are using a grill pan, put a plate on top of the sandwiches and top with something heavy, such as a pot. Or use a large frying pan and cook as you would grilled cheese sandwiches. This is delicious any way you cook it!

Cook until the sandwiches are golden brown, about 3 minutes. Cut the sandwiches in half and serve right away.

SERVES 4

¾ lb (375 g) day-old French bread or challah, cut into 1-inch (2.5-cm) slices

4 tablespoons (2 oz/60 g) unsalted butter, at room temperature

2 ripe bananas, sliced

⅓ cup (2 oz/60 g) plus 2 tablespoons semisweet chocolate chips

6 large eggs plus 2 yolks

2 cups (16 fl oz/500 ml) half-and-half or whole milk

1 cup (16 oz/250 g) sugar

1 teaspoon pure vanilla extract

CHOCOLATE CHIP & BANANA BREAD PUDDING

Spread one side of each bread slice with the butter. Lay half of the bread slices in the bottom of a 9-by-13-inch (23-by-33-cm) baking dish. Cut the bread slices to fit, as needed, covering as much of the bottom of the baking dish as possible. Top the bread slices with the bananas and ⅓ cup (2 oz/60 g) of the chocolate chips followed by the remaining bread slices. Sprinkle the remaining 2 tablespoons chocolate chips on top. Set aside.

In a large bowl, whisk together the eggs and yolks, half-and-half, sugar, and vanilla. Ladle the custard onto the bread, waiting to add more as needed until it's absorbed by the bread. Let the bread pudding stand at room temperature, occasionally pressing the bread into the custard with a flat spatula, until the bread is thoroughly saturated, about 30 minutes.

Preheat the oven to 350°F (180°C). Cover the bread pudding loosely with aluminum foil and bake for 45 minutes. Remove the foil and bake until the top is golden brown and the custard is set, about 20 minutes longer.

Let cool for 15 minutes. Using a knife, cut the pudding into squares. Use a spatula to scoop out the squares and serve.

SERVES 8–10

HOMEY COMFORT

Warm bread pudding just out of the oven is the ultimate comfort food. This recipe is a great way to use up leftover bread and extra-ripe bananas. You could also use raspberries or dried fruit, such as chopped cherries or apricots. Top this dessert with a dollop of Fresh Rhubarb-Raspberry Sauce (page 114)—and a mug of milky tea or hot chocolate if you're feeling a little decadent.

3 cups (¾ lb/375 g) raspberries

2 tablespoons sugar

2 cups (16 fl oz/500 ml) heavy cream

6 meringue cookies, broken into pieces

RASPBERRY-MERINGUE PARFAIT

NO-BAKE EASE

Here's a recipe for those who don't want to bake. This beautiful dessert looks special, but it couldn't be easier to assemble. Instead of the raspberry purée, you can use Fresh Rhubarb-Raspberry Sauce (page 114). Because there is no perfect way to build a parfait and no cooking involved, this is a great dessert to let the kids make.

Combine 2 cups (½ lb/250 g) of the raspberries and 1 tablespoon of the sugar in the blender and purée until well combined. Set aside.

In a large metal bowl, whip the heavy cream until soft peaks form. Add the remaining 1 tablespoon sugar and whip until stiff peaks form. Set aside.

Assemble the parfaits in wineglasses, Mason jars, or juice glasses. Divide half of the whipped cream evenly among the glasses, followed by half of the raspberry purée. Top with the cookies, dividing them evenly, and the remaining whipped cream and raspberry purée, again dividing them evenly. Scatter the remaining 1 cup (¼ lb/125 g) raspberries on top. Serve at once.

SERVES 4

MENUS

From Monday night soccer practice to family game night on Friday, putting together a delicious, balanced dinner on a weeknight schedule is made easier with these menus as a guide. For more tips on planning quick meals, see page 11.

MEATLESS FEAST

Plant-based proteins and nutrient-rich vegetables help start the week off on a healthy note.

QUINOA SALAD WITH ROASTED CARROTS & BLOOD ORANGES (page 21)
LEMON-THYME GRANITA (page 113)
FOR THE KIDS & ADULTS Seltzer with lemon slices

COMFORT FOOD NIGHT

Sink your forks into these classics. Assemble the bread pudding when prepping dinner, then let it bake while you eat.

CLASSIC MEAT LOAF WITH ROSEMARY-ROASTED VEGETABLES (page 97)
CHOCOLATE CHIP & BANANA BREAD PUDDING (page 119)
FOR THE ADULTS Red wine
FOR THE KIDS Sparkling apple juice

BREAKFAST ALL-AROUND

Everyone will like this menu, and it's supereasy to assemble. Have the kids squeeze the orange juice.

SMOKED SALMON OMELET WITH MIXED HERB SALAD (page 45)
ORANGE-MASCARPONE TOASTS WITH BLUEBERRIES & HONEY (page 111)
FOR THE ADULTS Prosecco
FOR THE KIDS Fresh-squeezed orange juice

GAME NIGHT

Finger food makes for even more fun on family game night.

SCOOPABLE HUEVOS RANCHEROS WITH TOMATILLO SALSA (page 39)
HOMEMADE CHOCOLATE PUDDING WITH STRAWBERRY DIPPERS (page 117)
FOR THE ADULTS Beer
FOR THE KIDS Old-fashioned root beer

MEDITERRANEAN NIGHT

This meal rounds up dishes inspired by Spain, France, and Greece, each using only a handful of ingredients!

SPANISH TORTILLA WITH CHORIZO (page 54)
MUSSELS MARINIÈRE (page 58)
APPLE FILO TART (page 112)
FOR THE ADULTS White wine
FOR THE KIDS Cranberry spritzers

CALM THE CHAOS

Make-ahead dishes are the way to go when time is tight. This hearty chili is a complete meal on its own.

QUINOA & BLACK BEAN CHILI (page 76)
FRESH RHUBARB-RASPBERRY SAUCE WITH ICE CREAM (page 114)
FOR THE KIDS & ADULTS Sparkling lemonade

INDEX

weldon**owen**

1045 Sansome Street, Suite 100, San Francisco, CA 94111

www.weldonowen.com

SCHOOL NIGHT

Conceived and produced by Weldon Owen, Inc.
In collaboration with Williams-Sonoma, Inc.
3250 Van Ness Avenue, San Francisco, CA 94109

A WELDON OWEN PRODUCTION

Copyright © 2015 Weldon Owen, Inc.
and Williams-Sonoma, Inc.

All rights reserved, including the right of
reproduction in whole or in part in any form.

Printed and bound in China by 1010 Printing, Ltd.

First printed in 2015
10 9 8 7 6 5 4 3 2 1

Library of Congress Cataloging-in-Publication
data is available.

ISBN 13: 978-1-61628-958-4
ISBN 10: 1-61628-958-9

Weldon Owen is a division of
BONNIER

WELDON OWEN, INC

President & Publisher Roger Shaw
SVP, Sales & Marketing Amy Kaneko
Finance Manager Philip Paulick

Associate Publisher Amy Marr
Associate Editor Emma Rudolph

Creative Director Kelly Booth
Senior Production Designer Rachel Lopez Metzger

Production Director Chris Hemesath
Associate Production Director Michelle Duggan

Director of Enterprise Systems Shawn Macey
Imaging Manager Don Hill

Photographer Erin Kunkel
Food Stylist Erin Quon
Prop Stylist Emma Star Jensen

ACKNOWLEDGMENTS

Weldon Owen wishes to thank the following people for their generous support in producing this book:
David Bornfriend, Gloria Geller, Marisa Kwek, Carolyn Miller, Elizabeth Parson, Sharon Silva, and Jane Tunks